First World War
and Army of Occupation
War Diary
France, Belgium and Germany

30 DIVISION
Divisional Troops
Machine Gun Corps
30 Battalion
1 March 1918 - 18 September 1919

WO95/2323/5

The Naval & Military Press Ltd
www.nmarchive.com
Published in association with The National Archives

Published by

The Naval & Military Press Ltd

Unit 10 Ridgewood Industrial Park,

Uckfield, East Sussex,

TN22 5QE England

Tel: +44 (0) 1825 749494

www.naval-military-press.com

www.nmarchive.com

War Diary	Mt. Vidaigne	08/09/1918	26/09/1918
War Diary	Mt. Kemmel	27/09/1918	30/09/1918
Heading	Appendix of War Diary for 30th Battalion Machine Gun Corps for the month of September 1918 Volume 5 1-30 September		
Operation(al) Order(s)	Operation Order No. 25. by Major O.M. Parker Temporally Commanding 30th Battalion Machine Gun Corps.	03/09/1918	03/09/1918
Operation(al) Order(s)	30th Battalion Machine Gun Corps Order No. 26	05/09/1918	05/09/1918
Operation(al) Order(s)	30th Battalion Machine Gun Corps Order No. 27	07/09/1918	07/09/1918
Operation(al) Order(s)	30th Battalion Machine Gun Corps Order No. 28	08/09/1918	08/09/1918
Operation(al) Order(s)	30th Battalion Machine Gun Corps Order No. 29	09/09/1918	09/09/1918
Operation(al) Order(s)	Amendment to 30th Battalion Machine Gun Corps Order No. 33	22/09/1918	22/09/1918
Operation(al) Order(s)	30th Battalion Machine Gun Corps Order No. 33	19/09/1918	19/09/1918
Heading	War Diary of 30th Battalion Machine Gun Corps for the Month of October 1918		
War Diary	Messines	01/10/1918	01/10/1918
War Diary	Wytschaete	02/10/1918	16/10/1918
War Diary	Hollebeke. Sheet. 28	16/10/1918	17/10/1918
War Diary	Roncq. Sheet 28	18/10/1918	19/10/1918
War Diary	Croise	20/10/1918	20/10/1918
War Diary	Sterhoek (Sheet 29.)	21/10/1918	21/10/1918
War Diary	Meuleken	22/10/1918	30/10/1918
War Diary	Rolleghem	31/10/1918	31/10/1918
Heading	Appendix to War Diary of 30th Battalion Machine Gun Corps for the month of October 1918 Volume. 1-31 Oct. 1918		
Operation(al) Order(s)	30th Battalion Machine Gun Corps Order No. 39 Appendix 1	02/10/1918	02/10/1918
Operation(al) Order(s)	Amendment To 30th Battalion Machine Gun Corps Warning Order No. 40 Appendix 2 (a)	05/10/1918	05/10/1918
Operation(al) Order(s)	30th Battalion Machine Gun Corps Order No. 41 Appendix 3 Appendix 3	09/10/1918	09/10/1918
Operation(al) Order(s)	30th Battalion Machine Gun Corps Order No. 42	10/10/1918	10/10/1918
Operation(al) Order(s)	30th Battalion Machine Gun Corps Order No. 43 Appendix 5	11/10/1918	11/10/1918
Miscellaneous	30th Battalion Machine Gun Corps.	21/08/1918	21/08/1918
Miscellaneous	A Short History of The Part Played By The 30th Battalion Machine Gun Corps In The Capture of The Dranoutre Ridge And The Advance Of August/September, 1918		
Operation(al) Order(s)	30th Battalion Machine Gun Corps Order No. 36	26/09/1918	26/09/1918
Operation(al) Order(s)	30th Battalion Machine Gun Corps Order No. 35	23/09/1918	23/09/1918
Operation(al) Order(s)	30th Battalion Machine Gun Corps Order No. 37	28/09/1918	28/09/1918
Miscellaneous	Appendix "A"		
Diagram etc	Appendix A Consolidation Areas		
Diagram etc	Appendix B		
Miscellaneous	Appendix "B" Barrage Organization Scheme To 30th Battalion Machine Gun Corps Order No. 43		
Miscellaneous	Addendum To 30th Battalion Machine Gun Corps Order No. 43	12/10/1918	12/10/1918
Operation(al) Order(s)	30th Battalion Machine Gun Corps Warning Order No. 44 Appendix 6	14/10/1918	14/10/1918
Operation(al) Order(s)	30th Battalion Machine Gun Corps Order No. 45 Appendix 7	15/10/1918	15/10/1918

Operation(al) Order(s)	30th Battalion Machine Gun Corps Order No. 46 Appendix 8	15/10/1918	15/10/1918
Operation(al) Order(s)	30th Battalion Machine Gun Corps Order No. 49 Appendix 9	26/10/1918	26/10/1918
Operation(al) Order(s)	30th Battalion Machine Gun Corps Order No. 50 Appendix 10	26/10/1918	26/10/1918
Operation(al) Order(s)	Amendment No. 1. To 30th Battalion Machine Gun Corps Order No. 50 Appendix (10a)	27/10/1918	27/10/1918
Miscellaneous			
Heading	War Diary of 30th Battalion Machine Gun Corps for the month of November 1918 Volume VI 1-30 Nov. 1918		
War Diary	Rolleghem	01/11/1918	04/11/1918
War Diary	Belleghem	05/11/1918	08/11/1918
War Diary	Heestert	09/11/1918	09/11/1918
War Diary	Watripont	10/11/1918	10/11/1918
War Diary	Bruyere	11/11/1918	13/11/1918
War Diary	Ellezelles	14/11/1918	14/11/1918
War Diary	Renaix	15/11/1918	15/11/1918
War Diary	Avelghem	16/11/1918	16/11/1918
War Diary	Luinghe (Near Mouscron)	17/11/1918	26/11/1918
War Diary	Luinghe	27/11/1918	27/11/1918
War Diary	La Vignette	28/11/1918	28/11/1918
War Diary	Croix Au Bois	29/11/1918	29/11/1918
War Diary	Bac St Maur	30/11/1918	30/11/1918
Heading	Appendix for War Diary of 30th Battalion Machine Gun Corps for the month of November 1918 Volume VI 1-30-11-18		
Operation(al) Order(s)	30th Battalion Machine Gun Corps Order No. 53 Appendix 1	05/11/1918	05/11/1918
Operation(al) Order(s)	Amendment No. 1 To 30th Battalion Machine Gun Corps Order No. 53	06/11/1918	06/11/1918
Operation(al) Order(s)	Amendment No. to 30th Battalion Machine Gun Corps Order No. 53	07/11/1918	07/11/1918
Miscellaneous	VR/G/700 Appendix 2	09/11/1918	09/11/1918
Operation(al) Order(s)	30th Battalion Machine Gun Corps Warning Order No. 55 Appendix 3	09/11/1918	09/11/1918
Operation(al) Order(s)	30th Battalion Machine Gun Corps Order No. 56 Appendix 4	09/11/1918	09/11/1918
Operation(al) Order(s)	30th Battalion Machine Gun Corps Order No 57 Appendix 5	10/11/1918	10/11/1918
Operation(al) Order(s)	30th Battalion Machine Gun Corps Order No. 58 Appendix 6	13/11/1918	13/11/1918
Operation(al) Order(s)	30th Battalion Machine Gun Corps Order No. 59 Appendix 7	14/11/1918	14/11/1918
Operation(al) Order(s)	30th Battalion Machine Gun Corps Order No. 60 Appendix 8	15/11/1918	15/11/1918
Operation(al) Order(s)	30th Battalion Machine Gun Corps Order No. 61 Appendix 9	16/11/1918	16/11/1918
Miscellaneous	30th Battalion Machine Gun Corps Order No. 62 Appendix 10	27/11/1918	27/11/1918
Operation(al) Order(s)	30th Battalion Machine Gun Corps Order No. 33 Appendix 11	22/11/1918	22/11/1918
Miscellaneous	30th Battalion Machine Gun Corps Order No. 64 Appendix 12	29/11/1918	29/11/1918

Heading	War Diary of 30th Battalion Machine Gun Corps for the month of December 1918 Volume VII 1-31 December 1918		
War Diary	St. Floris.	01/12/1918	01/12/1918
War Diary	Staple.	02/12/1918	31/12/1918
Heading	Appendix to War Diary of 30th Battalion Machine Gun Corps for the month of December 1918 Volume VII 1-31-12-18		
Operation(al) Order(s)	30th Battalion Machine Gun Corps Order No. 65 Appendix 1	30/11/1918	30/11/1918
Operation(al) Order(s)	30th Battalion Machine Gun Corps Order No. 66 Appendix 2	01/12/1918	01/12/1918
Heading	30th Battalion Machine Gun Corps. War Diary-Volume VII January 1919		
War Diary	Staple (Hazebrouck) 5a	01/01/1919	04/01/1919
War Diary	La Lacque	05/01/1919	18/01/1919
War Diary	Ambleteuse	19/01/1919	31/01/1919
Heading	30th Battalion Machine Gun Corps Appendices to War Diary Vol VII January 1919		
Operation(al) Order(s)	30th Battalion Machine Gun Corps Order No. 68 Appendix I	17/01/1919	17/01/1919
Operation(al) Order(s)	30th Battalion Machine Gun Corps Order No. 37 Appendix II	03/01/1919	03/01/1919
War Diary	Ambleteuse	01/02/1919	01/02/1919
War Diary	St Leonards. (Boulogne)	28/02/1919	28/02/1919
Heading	War Diary of 30th Bn Machine Gun Corps S February 1919		
Miscellaneous	Headquarters, 30th. British Division "G"	17/04/1919	17/04/1919
Miscellaneous	'A' Passed	18/04/1919	18/04/1919
War Diary	St. Leonards.	01/03/1919	31/03/1919
War Diary	Henriville	01/04/1919	27/04/1919
Miscellaneous	Headquarters, 30th. Division "G"	01/06/1919	01/06/1919
War Diary	Henriville	01/05/1919	30/05/1919
Miscellaneous	Headquarters. 30th Division "G"	07/07/1919	07/07/1919
War Diary	Ecault.	01/06/1919	24/06/1919
Miscellaneous	Headquarters, 30th Division "G"	04/08/1919	04/08/1919
War Diary	Ecault.	01/08/1919	15/08/1919
Miscellaneous	War Diaries of 30th Bn. Machine Gun Corps.	22/10/1919	22/10/1919
Miscellaneous	Headquarters, Boulogne Base, France	12/10/1919	12/10/1919
War Diary	Ecault Camp. Boulogne	01/08/1919	26/08/1919
War Diary	Ecault Camp. Boulogne.	01/09/1919	12/09/1919
War Diary	Shorncliffe	13/09/1919	18/09/1919

30 DIVISIONAL TROOPS

30 BN. MACHINE GUN CORPS

1918 MAR — 1919 SEPT

30th Div.

WAR
DIARY

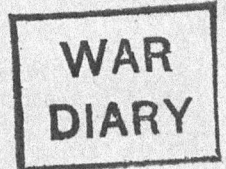

30th BATTALION, MACHINE GUN CORPS.

M A R C H

1 9 1 8

War Diary

of

30th Machine Gun Battalion

for month of

March 1918.

VOLUME I
for
March, 1918
p 1

Instructions regarding War Diaries and Intelligence Summaries are contained in F. S. Regs., Part II. and the Staff Manual respectively. Title pages will be prepared in manuscript.

WAR DIARY or ~~INTELLIGENCE SUMMARY.~~ of 30th Battalion Machine Gun Corps

(Erase heading not required.)

Army Form C. 2118.

0 88.

Place	Date	Hour	Summary of Events and Information	Remarks and references to Appendices
St QUENTIN AREA	1.3.18		A fine day, dry & cold. Administration of M. G. Coys passed from Brigade to Commdg Officer 30th Bn. M.G.C. Battalion created as 30th Batt. Machine Gun Corps. Companies formed as follows: No 21 Coy becomes "A" Coy. No 89 Coy becomes B Coy. No 90 Coy becomes C Coy. No 226 Coy becomes D Coy.	[initials]

Roll of Officers on Strength of Bn as follows:

Bn H.Q.

Lieut Col H. Blackwood M.C. Commdg.
Capt J. Mulligan M.C. 2/c Command.
Capt MacDermott M.C. Adjt.
Lieut Marshall Transport Off.
" Roberts A/Qr. Mr.

Companies.

Capt Tonge Commdg A Coy
" Rodbaugh M.C. " B "
" McPherson D.C.M. " C "
" Ward " D "
Lieut R. Bernhard 2/c Com A Coy
" A. W. Ashley Sec Off. A Coy
" C. D. Armstrong " A Coy
" J. E. Cumming Trans Off. A Coy
" A. L. Hutchinson Sec Off. A Coy
Capt H. K. Boyle 2/c Comd. D Coy

Lieut D. A. Dwest Sec Off. D Coy
" A. McColl Trans Off. D Coy
" P. L. Stokeley 2/c Com B Coy
" W. G. Bolans Sec Off. B Coy
" W. A. Kingston Sec Off. B Coy
" J. H. Gordon Sec Off. B Coy
" B. H. Wood Trans Off. B Coy
" H. C. Watham 2/c Com. C Coy
" F. C. Nicol Sec Off. C Coy
" C. J. Kenny Trans Off. C Coy
" W. W. Peters Sec. Off. C Coy
2/Lieut H. Hayles S.S. Off. A Coy
" R. A. Lunnes S.S. Off. A Coy
" H. Field S.S. Off. A Coy
" D. G. Diplock Sec Off. D Coy
" H. R. van H. Hunt Sec Off. D Coy
" H. B. Morrison Sec Off. D Coy

2/Lieut W. J. Haworth S.S. Off. D Coy
" W. H. Curtis Sec Off. D Coy
" R. Prentice S.S. Off. D Coy
" J. P. A. O'Regan Intell Off. (D Coy)
" W. Locke S.S. Off. B Coy
" H. T. Morgan S.S. Off. B Coy
" H. E. Clarke Sec Off. C Coy
" J. Donald Sec Off. C Coy
" G. A. Lindsay S.S. Off. C Coy
" A. M. Dunham S.S. Off. C Coy
" J. H. Lyndsay S.S. Off. C Coy
" E. Leeks S.S. Off. B Coy

Distribution of Batt is as follows: Bn Hd-Qrs & Transport at DOUCHY. A Coy ½ ETREILLERS in Battle Zone ½ at DOUCHY for Employment with Reserve Brigade. B Coy Forward Section Right with Coy Hd-Qrs at EPINE d'ALLON. C Coy Forward Sectn Left with Coy H.Q. on Manchester Hill. D Coy in Battle Zone with Hd-Qrs at ETREILLERS. A quiet uneventful 24 hrs in the whole area. Improvement to Billet Area carried out & organisation of Battalion proceeded with. Casualties – NIL. Strength of Batt 45 Officers [illegible] Ranks

D. D. & L., London, E.C.
(A8001) Wt. W1771/M2031 750,000 5/17 Sch. 52 Forms C2118/14

Instructions regarding War Diaries and Intelligence Summaries are contained in F. S. Regs., Part II. and the Staff Manual respectively. Title pages will be prepared in manuscript.

VOLUME I
for March, 1918
p.2.

WAR DIARY OF 30TH BATTALION MACHINE GUN CORPS.
or
~~INTELLIGENCE~~ SUMMARY.

(Erase heading not required.)

Army Form C. 2118.

Place	Date	Hour	Summary of Events and Information	Remarks and references to Appendices
St. QUENTIN AREA	2.3.18		A fine day, cold. Capt Tonge, A Coy to U.K. Lieut Bachrach assumes Temp. Command of A Coy. A quiet 24 hours in area. Organisation of Batt proceeded with & local improvements in Billet area carried out. Artificer Sgt. posted & joined Batt. Transport establishment completed and surplus Transport withdrawn. Sick NIL. Casualties NIL. Strength of Batt 45 Officers Other Ranks	[illegible]
St. QUENTIN AREA	3.3.18		A stormy day, Snow and Wind throughout the day. A quiet 24 hours in the Line. Sick NIL Casualties NIL Strength of Batt. 45 Officers Other Ranks	[illegible]
St. QUENTIN AREA	4.3.18		A rainy day. Distribution as heretofore. A quiet 24 hours in the Line. Capt & Q.M. Pearce joined for duty. Medical Officer posted (Lt O'Brien, U.S.R.) Organisation of Batt proceeded with and local improvements in area carried out. Sick NIL. Casualties NIL Strength of Batt. 45 Officers Other Ranks. 1 Med Off. Attached	[illegible]
St QUENTIN AREA	5.3.18		A rainy day during early hours of morning. Enemy raided in front of B Coy. However an uneventful 24 hours in the Line. Hostile Planes over DOUCHY area during night. Organisation of Batt proceeded with. Further improvements of area carried out. Batt Canteen opened. Sick NIL Casualties NIL Strength of Batt 45 Offs. Other Ranks.	[illegible]
St. QUENTIN AREA	6.3.18		A fine day, mild and bright. Aerial activity on both sides throughout the day. A quiet 24 hours in the Line. Organisation proceeded with. O.R. Room Sgt. Major arrived but taken on Strength. Sick NIL Casualties NIL Strength of Batt 45 Off. Other Ranks.	[illegible]
St QUENTIN AREA	7.3.18		A fine day, dull at periods. Organisation of Batt proceeded with. Batt found Working parties for R.F.A. Bays during day. Sgt W. Dean promoted C.S.M. C Coy. Lieut W. G. Bachrach and 1 O.R. from Leave. 2 O.R. to Leave. A quiet uneventful 24 hours in the area. Strength of Batt 45 Officers 810 Other Ranks. Batt Operation Order No 1 issued re Relief of Companies. Reinforcements of 5 O.R. from Base Depot. Posted to D Coy. Aerial activity during day & night.	[illegible]

D. D. & L., London, E.C. (A8001) Wt. W1771/M2031 750,000 5/17 Sch. 52 Forms C2118/14

VOLUME I
for
March 1918
p 3

Instructions regarding War Diaries and Intelligence Summaries are contained in F. S. Regs., Part II. and the Staff Manual respectively. Title pages will be prepared in manuscript.

WAR DIARY ~~or~~ ~~INTELLIGENCE SUMMARY.~~ OF 30TH BATTALION MACHINE GUN CORPS.

(*Erase heading not required.*)

Army Form C. 2118.

Place	Date	Hour	Summary of Events and Information	Remarks and references to Appendices
St. QUENTIN AREA	8.3.18		A fine day. In conjunction with Operation Orders No. 1 Inter-Coy Relief carried out. D Coy to Forward Zone. B Coy from Forward Zone to Battle Zone. Relief completed without incident at 2 a.m. [illegible] 4 O.R's posted to Bn from Inf Batt. Posted to A Coy. Working parties found for Fld. Aty. Bdes. A quiet uneventful 24 hours in area. 2/Lt. H. Thornton, [illegible] awarded the Albert Medal in Gold for gallantry in action EAST OF YPRES on 30.12.17. Sick Nil Casualties Nil Strength of Batt 45 Officers 814 Other Ranks	[illegible]
St QUENTIN AREA	9.3.18		A fine day. Mild and Bright. In conjunction with O.O. No 1 Inter Coy Relief carried out as follows. A Coy from DOUCHY Reserve area to Battle Zone & Forward Zone Left. C Coy from Forward Zone Left & ½ Battle Zone to DOUCHY Reserve. A quiet 24 hours in the area. Working parties found for R.A. 4 O.R's posted from Inf. Batt as Specialists. Sick NIL Casualties Nil. Strength of Batt. 45 Officers 818 Other Ranks. Allotment of Leave to U.K. 2 per Diem.	[illegible]
St. QUENTIN AREA	10.3.18		A fine day, mild and Bright. Aerial activity throughout the day. A quiet 24 hours in area. Working parties found for R.A. Improvements of locality of DOUCHY continued. Sick Nil Casualties Nil. Strength of Bn. 45 Officers 818 Other Ranks. 2 O.R's to Leave U.K.	[illegible]
St QUENTIN AREA.	11.3.18		A fine day, mild & bright. A quiet uneventful 24 hours in area. Improvements of locality continued. 2 O.R's to Leave. Sick NIL / Casualties Nil. 13 Pte Category "B" posted to fill vacancies in establishment from Area Empt. Coy. Strength of Batt 45 Officers 831 OR. Practice manning of Battle Zone carried out by teams billeted in DOUCHY. Battle Zone manned within 1 hr 15 minutes from time alarm given.	[illegible]
St. QUENTIN AREA.	12.3.18		A fine day. Warm and Bright. Aerial activity throughout day. Hostile Artillery more active than usual against Left Bde. Sector, otherwise a quiet, uneventful 24 hours in area. Training of Infantry Personnel commenced. Sick NIL Casualties Nil. 1 OR [illegible]. Lt. P.L. Stokley and 2/Lt H.L. Clark to Leave UK. Strength of Batt 45 Off 831 OR.	[illegible]

Instructions regarding War Diaries and Intelligence Summaries are contained in F. S. Regs., Part II. and the Staff Manual respectively. Title pages will be prepared in manuscript.

Army Form C. 2118.

VOLUME I for March 1918 p4

WAR DIARY OF 30TH BATTALION MACHINE GUN CORPS. ~~or INTELLIGENCE~~ SUMMARY.

(Erase heading not required.)

Place	Date	Hour	Summary of Events and Information	Remarks and references to Appendices
ST. QUENTIN AREA	13.3.18		A fine day, warm and bright. Aerial activity continues. Improvements to DOUCHY area carried on. Training of Infantry Personnel continues. A quiet uneventful 24 hours in area. 13 Category B men arrived. Taken on strength and posted to Companies. Sick NIL. Casualties NIL. Strength of Batt. 45 Off. 831 O.R. Six Guns moved into main line of resistance in Northern Bluyère Sector.	[illegible]
ST. QUENTIN AREA.	14.3.18.		A fine day, cold wind during forenoon. Warm and bright afternoon. Change in dispositions of Guns in forward Zone completed during night. Our Artillery active during night. Several fires and explosions noticed in hostile back areas in and about ST. QUENTIN. Aerial activity throughout afternoon. Otherwise a quiet uneventful 24 hours in Sector. Enemy very quiet. Sick NIL. Casualties NIL. Strength of Batt. 45 Officers. 831 Other Ranks.	[illegible]
ST. QUENTIN AREA	15.3.18		A fine day, bright and warm. Our aeroplanes active. Our artillery active during night. Very little retaliation on the part of the enemy. An uneventful 24 hours in the Sector. Lt. [illegible] joined from 35th M.G. Batt. Posted to and assumed command of "A" Coy. 2/Lieut. [illegible] & 13 [illegible] joined from Base Depot and posted to "A" Coy. 6 [illegible] joined from Base Depot. Taken on strength and posted to Companies. Sick NIL. Casualties NIL. Strength of Batt. 47 Officers 837 Other Ranks. Capt. McPherson rejoined from Leave U.K. Lt. [illegible] U.S.R. joined for duty as Medical Officer to Batt.	[illegible]
ST. QUENTIN AREA	16.3.18		A fine day, warm and bright. Aerial activity throughout day. Our artillery active during night. An uneventful 24 hours in the Sector. Sick NIL. Casualties NIL. Strength of Batt 47 Officers 837 other Ranks	[illegible]
ST. QUENTIN AREA	17.3.18		A fine day, bright and warm. Artillery carried out harassing fire during the night. A quiet uneventful 24 hours in the Sector. Sick NIL. Casualties NIL. Strength of Batt. 47 Officers 837 Other Ranks. Capt. H. K. Boyle rejoined from Course.	

D. D. & L., London, E.C. (A8004) Wt. W1771/M2031 750,000 5/17 Sch. 52 Forms/C2118/14

Instructions regarding War Diaries and Intelligence Summaries are contained in F. S. Regs., Part II. and the Staff Manual respectively. Title pages will be prepared in manuscript.

VOLUME I for March 1918 p5.

WAR DIARY or ~~INTELLIGENCE SUMMARY.~~ of 30TH BATTALION MACHINE GUN CORPS

(Erase heading not required.)

Army Form C. 2118.

Place	Date	Hour	Summary of Events and Information	Remarks and references to Appendices
ST. QUENTIN AREA	18.3.18.		A fine day, bright and warm. Aerial activity throughout day. Our artillery active during night. One big fire observed in Cattle Back area N. of ST QUENTIN which burnt for about 3 hours, many minor explosions occurring. The M.G's carried out harassing fire during night, 1180 rounds being fired on selected targets. A quiet uneventful 24 hours in the Line. Improvement of locality and training of recently joined personnel carried out in Back Areas. 38 O.R's from 17 Entrenching Batt. joined the Batt having been posted on selection for transfer to M.G.C. 38 O.R's from 17 Entrenching Batt joined M.G. Batt taken on strength and posted to Companies. They included 35 Bandsmen, complete with instruments and music. Batt Bath house opening and bathing carried out with great success. 1 O.R. from Base Depot joined, taken on strength and posted to "D" Coy. 2 Offs & 8 O.R. from Courses of Instruction. Strength of Batt 47 Officers 892 Oth. Ranks. Operation Orders No 2 issued re Inter-Coy Relief in the Line.	
ST. QUENTIN AREA	19.3.18.		A Wet day, clear for short periods. A quiet uneventful 24 hours in the area. Harassing fire by our Artillery and M.G's carried out during the night. During afternoon Div. Gas Officer inspected S.B.R.'s of Batt & gave a short lecture on Defensive Gas Measures. Sick 1 O.R. to F.A. Casualties Nil. Strength of Batt 47 Officers 892 Oth. Ranks.	
ST. QUENTIN AREA	20.3.18		A wet day. Clear for short periods. Teams manning the Battle Zone. Information was received that enemy would probably attack early next morning. All preparations were made. Casualties NIL.	
ST. QUENTIN AREA	21.3.18		Very misty morning. At 4.40 a.m. an intense enemy bombardment of great depth of forward & Battle Zones which preceded an enemy infantry attack at about 8 a.m. This attack was made in great numbers, and under cover of the mist [illegible] the enemy over-ran & [illegible] the Forward Zone, and as far as the Battle Zone. Casualties 13 Offs.	

D. D. & L., London, E.C. (A8004) Wt. W1771/M2031 750,000 5/17 Sch. 52 Forms/C2118/14

Instructions regarding War Diaries and Intelligence Summaries are contained in F. S. Regs., Part II. and the Staff Manual respectively. Title pages will be prepared in manuscript.

VOLUME I
for
March, 1918
P6

WAR DIARY of 30TH BATTALION MACHINE GUN CORPS
or
~~INTELLIGENCE SUMMARY.~~
(*Erase heading not required.*)

Army Form C. 2118.

Place	Date	Hour	Summary of Events and Information	Remarks and references to Appendices
	22.3.18		Enemy attack continued with great violence and guns were forced to retire from Battle Zone fighting a rearguard action to HAM. Casualties.	
	23.3.18		10 guns were in action in defence of HAM, but being greatly outnumbered and surrounded were compelled to evacuate. Casualties 1 Off.	
	24.3.18		The rearguard action continued to Moyencourt where the French rendered great assistance. Casualties 2 Offs. Details retired from Moyencourt to Roiglise.	
	25.3.18		Owing to casualties, loss of guns, etc, only 3 guns remained in action and they retired with the infantry, who had by now been relieved by the French. Casualties 1 Off. Remainder of Batt retired to Plessier.	
	26.3.18		Guns were in action at Bouchoir, Folies, Warvillers and Caesny.	
	27.3.18		Batt moved to Braches.	
	28.3.18		Batt moved to Rouvrel and the Division was formed into a composite Brigade No. 90 each Brigade being formed with a composite Batt and M.G. Batt working with 90 Composite Bde.	
	29.3.18		Batt at Rouvrel.	
	30.3.18		Batt marched to Saleux and entrained for St Valery.	
	31.3.18		Batt moved from St Valery to Ochancourt.	

1-4-18

[signature] Maj
Comdg 30 Bn MGC

D. D. & L., London, E.C.
(A8001) Wt. W1771/M2031 750,000 5/17 Sch. 52 Forms/C2118/14

12488, King L'pool Reg.
Later
142 Machine Gun
Coy

W. S. Andrew
c/o Mr A. J. Libbitts
Fruit Ridge Farm
Farmington
U. S. A
Michigan.

26/ar/[illegible]/40?

Having heard that information regarding what occurred in March 1918 on the battle front occupied by the Fifth Army was acceptable I beg to forward what happened in the St Quentin sector, being a member of 30th Machine Gun Batt. 30th Division taken prisoner March 21st 1918

Account as follows

Half of the 30th M. G. Batt, 32 guns occupied the line immediatly opposite St Quentin Cathedral in a village called Dallas, [? Sallon] 400 yards behind the front line, held by the 90th Brigade. The date of taking over was the 7th March 1918, so we were exactly 14 days in this position before the German attack

2/

The canal ran between us and the enemy, but was drained by him ~~no~~ near the town, and was practically a dry bed, & there were also a network of trenches dug long before by the French troops extending on both sides of the canal & barricaded near to the German lines. I am stating this as they advanced up these communication trenches that morning. Speaking for the 90th Brig, it was under strength to that extent that the front line force was skeleton consisting of isolated Lewis Gun posts, to say nothing of inexperienced personnel, however gallant they were

3/

On Wednesday evening the 20th March the enemy sent over a number of both scout & battle planes about 6 o/c & by drawing fire from our gun positions had them "spotted." I wish to mention here that not more than 3 or 4 of our Vickers were in concrete positions or shelters, the remainder being only camouflaged by branches &c. The section that I belonged to commanded by 2nd Lieut. Morrison had 1 gun in concrete emplacement on a 40 ft bluff above the village, Dallas, Dallon, and the other gun of course was in the open on top, covered as well as possible. We had a tunnel to the concrete position that sheltered the section, 12 men, or would never have got into action. That " night the heavy batteries, 6" & 8 shelled St Quentin, & exploded a huge amount of shells that were massed there even in the open showing what preparations the enemy had been making; it is also worth mentioning that the Huns did not reply to our fire, or even send one shell for the whole 14 days & that grass a foot high was growing in shellholes made 2 or 3 years previously or possibly the first year of the war. When the "Boche" planes came over the

5/

previous evening a small squadron of our aviators went over to engage them, I am not sure of the number but not over six (6). It was a forlorn hope, for none came back, the German "planes rising from the city & engaging 2 & 3 to one in an almost desperate move to stop them at all cost. The German barrage opened as nearly as I can place it at 5. a.m. 21st March on Thursday, & included an enormous amount of gas shells & every calibre they possessed, making of course a creeping barrage in a crescent shaped attack. All wires being destroyed Mr Morrison sent a message to headquarters, but the runner was killed in 30 yards. The next thing we heard the fighting in the front line & went into action in the open, though we had been firing from the end of the tunnel at 800 - 1000 yds. By good luck, the other gun was intact & we started in with a full crew, except 1 casualty, the runner. 2 ~~4~~ men on each gun, the remainder ~~a~~ using rifles, range 400 yds in clear view, but some of the enemy had to cross the canal, & ~~try~~ make pontoons or use scows. The others crossed the dry canal bed & came up the deep trenches. While sighting on the scows, I noticed that many

7/

of the attackers wore the spiked helmet (Pickelhauber) as in 1914, & seemed to be picked troops, from their actions. A group of them boarded as a scow, were all killed or wounded, & new men took their place. I can safely say that Mr Morrison's section held up the Hun advance on this sector & inflicted heavy casualties on the enemy. They sent a strong bombing party to our rear, & being occupied with firing to the front, the first Hun bomber got within 20 yards of me before I turned. However, we wiped out the bombing party, but had 5 more casualties & 1 Vickers

8/

put out of action. Mr Morrison emptied his revolver, & we used the Mills grenades, only half of which exploded, by the way. Morrison swung the gun around & we used our last 2 belts in a circle (500 rounds), the smoke being so thick that we could not distinguish the enemy, but knew he was all round us. Then stripped the gun, & threw the lock away. Morrison ordered me to take care of our wounded man, the others were dead & try & get him out. He took 3 men in a dash for the rear position to get into action there. I had 1 man named O'Connor, to assist

9

me with the wounded man, leg shattered by bomb. I carried this man on my shoulders with the other man assisting me for perhaps 200 yds down the board tracks, hoping to get through the barrage, (our own), leave the wounded man safe & push through to the rear to join up. As we crossed the commun. trench I slid the man off my back to rest on rising ground, & as I turned a German officer had me covered. The man with me O'Connor, was killed at the same time by our M. Gun fire from the rear of course unavoidably. This Hun officer had been held up in this trench with

10

his platoon by our barrage created by the heavies for the R.F.A. Batteries were among the first to be captured, how, I cannot say. This officer could speak excellent English, asked me a lot of questions & of course learned nothing, but it showed that he & his men had only arrived the night before & did not know whether they were near Amiens or any other city. As a matter of fact, this was 25 Kilo from Ham, Noyon, Nesle & those points. One of his N.C.O.s wanted to shoot me for a Machine Gunner, & showed they had lost heavily from our section, but I was sent back,

11

under escort to the German rear, which was in an awful state of confusion. The casualties had been heavy, they had no Medical Corps working in an efficient way. Their food rations were very poor, but between carrying a few wounded & waiting for an escort, it was 3 o/c in the afternoon before I reached the city & found Morrison & 3 men there, making 5 prisoners in our M.G. Section & 7 casualties. I heard on good authority that the German officers had distinct orders to take all unwounded men possible, & they killed the wounded on the ground. The following morning in St Quentin there were approximately 1800 N.C.O.'s & men and 250 officers of the Fifth army. A German officer acting interpreter, asked if any one of any rank cared to give details of rations issued to our men in the field & if they objected it was quite alright. An N.C.O. rank of sergeant told them 3/4 lb meat & all the usual stuff. They compared notes & were visibly impressed. The previous night, about 12 o/c, the German commander in St Quentin had granted the request of a Lt-Colonel of the 90th Brigade for some kind of rations for the men, & was only able to issue canned beef & water

13

but apologizing for the shortage in various ways, as the officer who made the request informed everybody by proxy. Yes, the German army at its best then was poorly equipped as to transport horses, stretchers, Field Ambulance, & food in any form.

This account is pro'ably belated & possibly ancient history but it is true.

Yours Truly

Wm. P. Andrew

142172, 30th Batt. M. Gun Corps

Late 12488 Kings Liverpool Reg

Intended for historical purpose.

Any communication to enclosed address will be received

Yours Sincerely

M.P.C. Andrew

Original | War Diary | Confidential

VR 2

of the

30th Machine Gun Battalion

For the month of April, 1918.

Volume No. 2 | 1-30 April, 1918.

30TH
BATTALION,
MACHINE GUN CORPS.
No. G910
Date 2 · 5 · 19.

Headquarters,

30th.British Division "G".

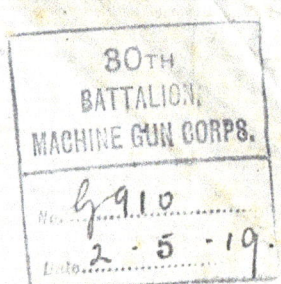

Herewith War Diary of this unit for the month of April please.

[signature]
Captain for Lieut-Colonel,
2/5/19. Commanding 30th.Battalion Machine Gun Corps.

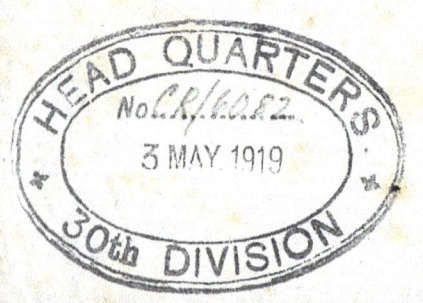

HEAD QUARTERS
No C.R./60.82
3 MAY 1919
30th DIVISION

Instructions regarding War Diaries and Intelligence Summaries are contained in F. S. Regs., Part II. and the Staff Manual respectively. Title pages will be prepared in manuscript.

WAR DIARY
of 30th Machine Gun Battalion.
~~INTELLIGENCE SUMMARY.~~

(Erase heading not required.)

Army Form C. 2118.

Place	Date	Hour	Summary of Events and Information	Remarks and references to Appendices
OCHANCOURT	1/4/18	-	30th Battalion M.G.C. in rest billets at OCHANCOURT. Reorganising and refitting proceeded with	ABBEVILLE 1/100,000
"	2/4/18	-	Reorganization carried on.	
"	3/4/18	-	Reorganization continued. Battn. H.Q. personnel detailed. Warning Order received for move Northwards into a Sector of the line. C.O. MAJOR J. MUHLIG, M.C. went on in advance to make all necessary arrangements.	
"	4/4/18.	2 P.M.	Battalion left OCHANCOURT and proceeded to WOINCOURT and FEUQUIERES and thence by rail to PROVEN and ROUSBRUGGE. For details of move see Battalion Order No: 4 2/LT. HUNT rejoined 'D' Company from leave.	APP. I
B 11 a. 4 0.	5/4/18		Battalion arrived in the ELVERDINGHE area. Billetted in CAMBRIDGE CAMP. B. 11 a. 4 0. C.O. made arrangement for relief with 1st Battalion. M.G.C.	Sheet 28 1/40,000
	6/4/18		Battalion prepared to go into the line. C.O., O.C. A & C reconnoitred the line North of POELCAPPELLE. LT. P. L. STOCKLEY and 2/LT. H. CLARKE rejoined B and C Companies respectively from leave. CAPT. H. K. BOYLE rejoined D Company from leave.	
		3 p.m.	Nos. 1 of Gun teams went into the line in advance.	
	7/4/18		44 Guns, tripods and spare parts arrived from Ordnance.	
		5.30 P.M.	2 Sections (8 Guns) of 'A' Company and 2 Sections (5 Guns) of 'B' Company under command of CAPT. FRASER M.C. (O.C. 'A' Company) left Cambridge Camp to go into the line and relieve 14 Guns of 1st Battalion M.G.C. 'C' Company (8 Guns) under command of CAPT. A. McPHERSON, D.C.M. left CAMBRIDGE CAMP to go into reserve in HUDDLESTONE CAMP For details of relief see Battalion Operation Order No. 5 Relief complete. Casualties - nil. Strength 30 Officers 620 O.R.	APP. II
B 11 a. 4 0.	8/4/18.		Quiet day. Casualties - nil.	
	9/4/18.		Nothing special to report. Casualties. nil.	
	10/4/18		Normal. Enemy artillery very active during the night on our back areas. Casualties - nil.	
	11/4/18		Normal. Enemy artillery very active during the night on our back areas. LT. KINGDOM relieved 2/LT. DONALD and 2/LT. MASON relieved 2/LT. PRENTICE in the Forward Zone. Casualties. - nil.	
	12/4/18		Normal. Fairly quiet 24 hours. One casualty. 1 O.R.	
	13/4/18		Normal. 'D' Company (12 Guns) under command of CAPT. E. E. WARD relieved 'A' Company in the Forward Zone. The 4 Forward Guns of 'A' Company being withdrawn to the Battle Zone. For particulars of relief see Operation Order No. 7 For disposition of Guns see Appendix Relief complete. Casualties - Nil	APP. III
B. 11. a. 4 0.	14/4/18.		Normal. Very cold with strong wind. Our Machine Guns fired 2.000 rounds harassing fire on night of 13/14.4.18. Casualties. Nil.	
B. 11. a. 4 0.	15/4/18		Normal. Front guns were withdrawn in accordance with orders. For details see Operation Order No. 9. Personnel of 'B' Company divided among A and D Companies as reinforcements, leaving the Battalion reorganized into 3 complete Companies of 16 Guns (A, C, & D).	

A5834 Wt. W4973/M687 750,000 8/16 D. D. & L. Ltd. Forms/C.2118/13.

Army Form C. 2118.

Instructions regarding War Diaries and Intelligence Summaries are contained in F. S. Regs., Part II. and the Staff Manual respectively. Title pages will be prepared in manuscript.

WAR DIARY
~~or~~
~~INTELLIGENCE SUMMARY.~~

(Erase heading not required.)

Place	Date	Hour	Summary of Events and Information	Remarks and references to Appendices
B 11 a. 4.0.	16/4/18		normal. Enemy artillery shelling our back areas heavily. Casualties - nil. Battalion less H.Q. moved to WHITE MILL CAMP ELVERDINGHE	
B. 14 d. 7. 8.	17/4/18		Guns in the line were relieved by Belgians. For details see Operation Order No: 10. Enemy were engaged and casualties inflicted. Harassing fire was carried out during the 24 hours. 40,000 rounds were fired. Casualties nil. A Company (less 1 Section) joined 89th Brigade and moved off under their orders to IX Corps.	Map SCh 28 app V
B. 14. d. 7. 8	18/4/18		Battalion (less A and D Companies) moved to ~~Camp~~ at G. 15 c. 0. 6. D Company went to 21st Bde. Battalion remained with 90th Bde. See Operation Order No: 11. Division in reserve to XXII Corps	App VI
G 15 c. 0.6 G. 22 a. 3 9.	19/4/18	7.30 AM	Battalion (less A and D Companies) moved to Camp at G 22 a 3. 9.	
		11 A.M.	Orders received to detail one Company to accompany 21st Composite Brigade if required. D Company was detailed	
		3 P.M.	Orders received for 20 Guns and teams to be got ready to go into the line with 21st Composite Brigade in the Sector in front of WERSTRAAT. 1 Section remaining from A Company consisting of personnel of B Company detailed to accompany D Company.	
			D Company (20 Guns) relieved 12 Guns of 9th Battn. M.G.C. between HILL 60 and EIKHOFF FARM. 8 Guns placed in reserve for the night at SPOIL BANK, pending selection of positions. D Company then came under orders of G.O.C. 21st Infantry Brigade, who were under orders of G.O.C. 21st Division.	
	20/4/18		C Company reorganised into 4 complete Sections. Positions reconnoitred for 16 guns in the OUDERDOM - BRANDHOEK line.	
	21/4/18		Positions mentioned above were started on by C. Company open emplacements and ammunition shelters made.	
	22/4/18		work on OUDERDOM line continued. A Company returned with 89th Infantry Brigade from BAILLEUL area. Their casualties had been 5 O.R. wounded. 'D' Company lost 1 O.R. killed & 1 O.R. wounded.	
	23/4/18		work on OUDERDOM line continued by 'C' Company. 'A' Company resting & reorganizing.	
	24/4/18		'C' Company detailed to move if needed with 89th Infantry Bde for counter attack purposes at 2 hours notice. 'A' Company continued work on emplacements.	
	25/4/18		'C' Company moved with 89th Bde Remainder of Battn moved to ERIC CAMP.	
	26/4/18		'A' Company joined 89th Bde.	
	27/4/18		Remainder of Battn (Headquarters & surplus Transport) moved to ST. MARIE CAPPEL en route for LEDERZEELE.	
	28/4/18		at Billet 141 N. 7 d. 2/8 refitting &c	
	29/4/18		at Billet 141 N. 7. d. 2/8 " "	
	30/4/18		LT. COL. MUHLIG & 2/LT O'REGAN moved to CASSEL for purposes of reconnoitring new line. Remainder of Battalion details stayed at Billet 141.	

J. MacLuim [?] Capt & Adjutant
for Lieut-Colonel
Commanding 30th Machine Gun Battalion

A5834 Wt. W4973/M687 750,000 8/16 D. D. & L. Ltd. Forms/C.2118/13.

Appendices

to

War Diary

of

30th Machine Gun Battalion

For the month of April, 1918

Volume No.   1-30 April 1918.

I

S E C R E T.

Copy No. ....

30th MACHINE GUN BATTALION ORDER No. 4.

April 3rd, 1918.

1. The 30th Machine Gun Battalion will move by rail on 4th & 5th March to the 2nd Army Area in accordance with the attached table.

2. The Division will probably go into the line on a Brigade front on April 6th/7th relieving the 1st Division in the POLECAPELLE Sector. Orders for the relief will be issued later.

3. Lieut. Nicol will report to Division Station Staff Officer at FEUQUIERES at 5.30 p.m., 4th inst., and 2nd Lieut. O'Regan to Division Station Staff Officer WOINCOURT at 3.30 p.m., 4th inst. They will act as entraining officers for the Battalion and will move with 3rd and 4th trains.

4. Company Officers' baggage and Company blankets will be as far as possible carried on the spare fighting limbers.

5. Grooms and chargers will accompany their respective officers.

6. Cooks, Watermen etc. will move with their respective vehicles.

7. Os. C., Companies will ensure that billets are left scrupulously clean.

8. The B.T.O. will arrange that the N.C.Os. are equally distributed among the four parties, and that breast ropes are provided, and are ready available for securing animals in the trucks.

9. PLEASE ACKNOWLEDGE.

[signature]

Captain & Adjutant
30th Machine Gun Battalion.

Copy No. 1 "A" Coy., 30th M.G. Bn.
2 "B" Coy., ""
3 "C" Coy., ""
4 "D" Coy., ""
5 Quartermaster ""
6 Bn. Transport Officer. ""
7 R.S.M. ""
8 Lieut. F.C. Nicol ""
9 2nd Lieut. O'Regan""
10 File
11 War Diary

IV

SECRET.   Copy No....

30th MACHINE GUN BATTALION ORDER No.6.

April 7th 1918.

1. The 30th Battalion, Machine Gun Corps will take over the Battle Zone positions in Divisional Area on 7th inst.

2. 8 gun teams and detachments, "C" Company, will move into HUDDLESTONE CAMP on 7th inst.
Move to be completed by 7.30 p.m.

3. Completion of move will be reported to Battalion H.Q. and to H.Q., 90th Infantry Brigade by runner.

4. ACKNOWLEDGE.

[signature]

Captain & Adjutant,
30th Machine Gun Battalion.

Issued at .....

Copy No. 1 O.C., "A" Coy., 30th M.G. Bn.
2 " "B" Coy., "
3 " "C" Coy., "
4 " "D" Coy., "
5 30th Division, "G".
6 90th Infantry Brigade.
7 89th Infantry Brigade.
8 1st Battalion, M.G.C.
9 War Diary.
10 File.

II

SECRET.

Copy No. 7..

WARNING ORDER No 6

April 5th 1918.

1. The Battalion will relieve the 1st Battalion in the line on the 7th/8th inst.

2. Dispositions of guns will be as follows:-

(a) Front System of Forward Zone .. .. .. 8 guns.
(b) Support System of Forward Zone .. .. 6 guns.
(c) Divisional Reserve .. .. 6 guns.

3. Relieving Companies will be as follows:-

(a) 8 guns of "A" Company under Captain Fraser, M.C. & 2 officers.
(b) } 12 guns "B" Coy.} Under Captain Macpherson, D.C.M. & 3 officers.
(c) } "C" Coy.}

4. C.O., Captain Fraser, Captain Macpherson, will reconnoitre area, and arrange details of relief on 6th inst, leaving CAMBRIDGE CAMP at 9 a.m..

5. Nos. 1 of each gun team of Forward Zone Guns (14 guns) will be prepared to move into the line at 4 p.m. 6th inst.

6. PLEASE ACKNOWLEDGE.

[signature]
Captain & Adjutant,
30th Machine Gun Battalion.

Copy No. 1 O.C., "A" Coy., 30th M.G. Bn.
2 "" "B" " ""
3 "" "C" " ""
4 "" "D" " ""
5 90th Infantry Brigade.
6 30th Division, "G".
7 War Diary.
8 File

111

Secret

30th Machine Gun Battalion

Operation Orders No 7.

Refce Maps

12th April 1918

1. Inter Company Reliefs will take place in accordance with the following Table.

2. Details of Relief will be arranged direct between O C Companies concerned; but there will be no movement E. of STEENBEEK before 7-30 P.M.

3. All defence schemes, Trench maps, Barrage Charts and Trench stores will be handed over and Receipts obtained, copies of which will be forwarded to Battalion Headquarters within 24 hours of completion of relief.

4. Completion of Relief will be reported to Battalion Headquarters 89th Brigade by Code word "WARDIN"

5. Please acknowledge.

COPIES:

1. 30. Divisional G.
2. 89th Brigade
3. A. Company, 30th Battn.
4. D " "
5. 90: Brigade } For information
6. 21: " }
7. B Company, 30: Bn. }
8. C. " "
9. War Diary.
10. File

Relief Table to accompany 30 Bn MGC O.O. No 7.

DATE	UNIT	FROM	TO	RELIEVING	REMARKS
1918 APRIL NIGHT 13th/14th.	'D' Company 30th Battn. MGC.	Divisional Reserve & Canal Defence	Forward System	A Company 30th Battn. MGC.	On relief A Coy move to CAMBRIDGE CAMP and will be DIV. RESERVE & CANAL DEFENCE

C128/6

IV

SECRET. Copy No. 6.

30th MACHINE GUN BATTALION ORDER No. 2.

Reference Maps Sheet 28 1/20,000
Sheet 28 1/20,000

April 15th 1918.

1. "D" Company, 30th Machine Gun Battalion will withdraw all guns, S.A.A. etc. from positions E. of the STEENBEEK on night of 15th/16th April.

2. Withdrawal will be completed as soon as possible after dark, but in any case all troops will be W. of the STEENBEEK by 4 a.m.

3. On withdrawal the dispositions of "D" Company will be as follows:-

2 Sections (8guns) in positions W. of STEENBEEK (now Forward Zone)
Remainder of Company and Company H.Q., CAMBRIDGE CAMP.

4. The 8 guns and teams etc. to occupy positions in FORWARD ZONE will rendezvous at Cross Roads C.9.d.30.70. and will be guided into positions by Guides from "C" Company.

5. O.C., "D" Company will report in person to O.C., 17th Bn., Kings Liverpool Regt. as soon as all personnel is W. of the STEENBEEK.

6. The positions to be taken up by the 2 Sections, "D" Coy. will be:

Nos. 11, 12, 13, 14, situated in squares 15.b. and 9.c., and four others which will be notified to teams at rendezvous.

2/Lt. Hoyle and four teams "A" Company should be in 11, 12, 13, 14, by 6 p.m. to-night.

On relief by four teams, "D" Company, they will return to CAMBRIDGE CAMP.

7. On completion of occupation Commander of FORWARD ZONE Machine Guns will devolve upon Lieut. Watkins, O.C., "C" Coy. with H.Q. at FUSILIER HOUSE.

8. ACKNOWLEDGE.

~~Captain & Adjutant,~~ Major
30th Machine Gun Battalion.

Copy No. 1 "A" Coy., 30th M.G. Bn.
2 "B" Coy., " "
3 "D" Coy., " "
4 2nd Lieut. Hoyle.
5 File [illegible]
✓ 6 War Diary.

S E C R E T.   Copy No......

30th MACHINE GUN BATTALION ORDER No. 10.

Ref. Maps: Sheets 20 S.W. & S.E.)
28 S.W.)
1/20,000)

April 17th 1918.

---

1. In conjunction with 30th Division Order No. 188 the 30th Battalion Machine Gun Corps will be relieved in the line by the 4th Belgian Infantry Division on night April 17th/18th

2. In connection with this Order "C" Company (24 guns) will be relieved as follows :-

   8 guns by 8th Company 10th Belgiann Infantry Regiment.
   8 guns by 12th Company 10th Belgian Infantry Regiment.
   2 guns by 12th Company 18th Belgian Infantry Regiment.
   6 guns by 4th Company 18th Belgian Infantry Regiment.

3. Details of relief have already been arranged between O.C., "C" Company, 30th M.G. Bn. and Os.C., Companies, Belgian Infantry.

4. All maps, aeroplane photographs and documents dealing with the sector will be handed over on relief.

5. Completion of relief will be notified by O.C., "C" Company to Battalion H.Q. and 90th Infantry Brigade by wiring code word "HALSTEAD".

6. On relief "C" Company will move to WHITE MILL CAMP, ELVERDINGHE.

7. The Battalion will be prepared to move to XXII Corps area by bus on 18th inst.

8. ACKNOWLEDGE.

J MacDermott

Captain & Adjutant,
30th Machine Gun Battalion.

Copy No. 1 "B" Coy., 30th M.G. Bn.
2 "C" Coy., "
3 "D" Coy., "
4 2nd i/Cmd., "
5 Q.M., "
6 T.O., "
7 90th Infantry Brigade
8 File
9 War Diary.

S E C R E T. OPERATION ORDER NO: 11.

by

MAJOR J. MUHLIG, M.C.

Commanding 30th Machine Gun Battalion.

12th April, 1918.

Reference Sheet 27 1/40,000.

1. In conjunction with O. 1160, 30th Battalion Machine Gun Corps will march to XXII Corps area today, April 12th, coming under the orders of the latter Corps on arrival in the Area.

2. For the purposes of the march and Billeting in the new area, Brigade Groups will be formed as follows:-

21st Infantry Brigade Group.

89th Infantry Brigade Group.

3. Letter "D" Company, complete with Transport, (including teams from the line) will be attached to 21st Infantry Brigade Group.

30th Machine Gun Battalion, (less two Companies) will be attached to 89th Brigade Group.

4. In the new area Headquarters 21st. Infantry Brigade will be established at H. 19. b. 3.9.

Headquarters 89th Infantry Brigade at G. 10.d.4.1.

5. The distances laid down, i.e. between Companies 100 yds; between Battalions 500 yds; between Units and Transport 100 yds, will be strictly observed on the march.

6. Billeting representatives "D" Company will meet Staff Captain 21st. Brigade at Headquarters 21st. Division, ROOGRAAF. G. 26. c. at 2-30p.m. today.

7. O.C. "D" Company will report in person to Brigade Major 21st. Brigade at WHITE MILL CAMP giving strength of Company, immediately on receipt of these orders.

8. Remainder of Battalion will be ready to move after 12 noon.

9. March Table attached.

10. ACKNOWLEDGE.

Captain & Adjutant.

30th MACHINE GUN BATTALION.

Copies to:

1. "B" Company 30th M. G. Bn.
2. "C" " "
3. "D" " "
4. 2nd in Command.
5. Q. M.
6. B. T. O.
7. 21st. Infantry Brigade } For information
8. 89th " " }
9. File.
10. War Diary.

MARCH TABLE ISSUED WITH 30TH DIVISION ORDER No. 169

SERIAL No.	DATE	UNIT OR FORMATION	FROM	TO	HEAD OF COLUMN TO PASS STARTING POINT		ROUTE
					TIME	PLACE	
1.	APRIL 18TH.	DIVNL. H.Q. GROUP	ELVERDINGHE CHATEAU	SCOTTISH CAMP H.23.b	9.30 A.M.	RD. JUNC. B.19.c	A.30. CENTRAL – LINDENGOES FME.
2.	–DO–	21ST INFY. BDE GROUP	WHITE MILL CAMP & ELVERDINGHE AREA	SQUARES G.21, 22, 27 & 28.	10. A.M		
3.	–DO–	90TH INFY BDE GROUP	ELVERDINGHE AREA	SQUARES G.10, 11 & 16.	3 p.m.		

Instructions regarding War Diaries and Intelligence Summaries are contained in F. S. Regs., Part II. and the Staff Manual respectively. Title pages will be prepared in manuscript.

Vol III for May 1918 p. 2.

WAR DIARY of 30th Machine Gun Battalion
or
~~INTELLIGENCE SUMMARY.~~
(Erase heading not required.)

Army Form C. 2118.

Vol 3

Place	Date	Hour	Summary of Events and Information	Remarks and references to Appendices
N.7.d.2.8. (Sheet 27)	1.5.18		30th Battalion M.G.C. disposed as follows:- Battalion H.Q. Details & Surplus Transport in LEDERZEELE area (N.7.d.2.8). Lieut. Col. [illegible] & 2nd Lt. O'Regan at CASSEL reconnoitring [illegible] lines in conjunction with VIII Corps. "A" Coy (11 guns) & "B" Coy (10 guns) in the line in KRUISSTRAATHOEK – RIDGEWOOD sector under 21st Division. "D" Coy (8 guns) in reserve at ERIE CAMP. Major J. A. Roxburgh in command of personnel in the line with 21st Division. JHR	
	2.5.18		In the evening "A" & "B" Coys were relieved by 16 guns of 19th Bn. M.G.C. Relief complete by 9.20 p.m. On relief "A" & "B" Coys came to ERIE CAMP. JHR	
	3.5.18		"A", "B" & "D" Coys reorganised into 2 Companies of 16 guns; "A" & "B" Coys under command of Majors Fraser & McPherson respectively. Surplus transport sent to Battalion Details at LEDERZEELE. 1 section "A" Coy under Lieut. [illegible] moved into the line into reserve on western edge of DICKEBUSCH LAKE. JHR	
	4.5.18		In the evening 12 guns of "B" Coy went into the line under Capt. Boyle in the KLEIN VIERSTRAAT sector, remainder in reserve at ERIE CAMP. JHR	
	5.5.18		1 section of "A" Coy in reserve at DICKEBUSCH LAKE relieved by 33rd Division. JHR	
	6.5.18		Normal Day. JHR	
	7.5.18		Nothing to report beyond usual artillery activity. JHR	
	8.5.18		Enemy put down a heavy barrage in the early morning followed by an infantry attack which took our front line & RIDGEWOOD. 4 guns were knocked out & several casualties sustained. The remaining guns obtained good targets & fired with effect. The situation was restored in the evening. "A" Coy (12 guns) relieved "B" Coy in the line. Some casualties were also sustained during the relief. 30th Division Composite Brigade relieved by 19th Brigade, 33rd Division. JHR	

A7092). Wt. W12839/M1293 750,000. 1/17. D. D & L., Ltd. Forms/C2118/14.

Instructions regarding War Diaries and Intelligence Summaries are contained in F. S. Regs., Part II. and the Staff Manual respectively. Title pages will be prepared in manuscript.

Vol III for May 1918 p. 1.

WAR DIARY of 30th Machine Gun Battalion
or
~~INTELLIGENCE SUMMARY.~~
(Erase heading not required.) (Contd.)

Army Form C. 2118.

Place	Date	Hour	Summary of Events and Information	Remarks and references to Appendices
N 7 d 2.8 (Chargy)	9.5.18		Normal day. In the evening C Coy was relieved by B Coy of 33rd Battalion M.G.C. Relief completed without casualties. On relief A & C Coys. concentrated at ERIE CAMP. FHR	
	10.5.18		In reserve at ERIE CAMP. FHR	
	11.5.18		H.Q. & C Coys. moved to N 7 d 2.8. Transport moving by road & personnel by bus. FHR	
	12.5.18		30th Bn. M.G.C. in rest billets at N 7 [illegible] FHR	
	13.5.18		13 Subalterns & 54 O.R. transferred to 31st Bn. M.G.C. [illegible] under orders of [illegible] Infantry [illegible] Transport Officer for disposal according to A.G's orders. FHR	
	14.5.18		Remainder of personnel moved by train to M.G.C. Base Depot [illegible] as reinforcements. Lieut-Col. [illegible] & small staff remain [illegible] 30th Division as Machine Gun adviser. FHR	

May 18th 1918

F.H. Roxburgh
Major
Commanding 30th Machine Gun Battn.

A7092). Wt. W12839/M1293 750,000. 1/17. D, D & L., Ltd. Forms/C2118/14.

Secret

Appendix to

War Diary

of 'A' Battalion Machine Gun Corps

For the month of June 1918

Appendix II

30 Bn M G Corps

Secret

Original

Vol 4

War Diary

of "A" Battalion Machine Gun Corps

For the Month of June 1918

Volume II

Army Form C. 2118.

Instructions regarding War Diaries and Intelligence Summaries are contained in F. S. Regs., Part II. and the Staff Manual respectively. Title pages will be prepared in manuscript.

WAR DIARY
or
INTELLIGENCE SUMMARY.

(Erase heading not required.)

Place	Date	Hour	Summary of Events and Information	Remarks and references to Appendices
PONT REMY.	1/6/18	10-15 -11am	Officers Class started in Physical Training and Bayonet Fighting under Acting C.S.M. Bradman. Work cleaning of Saddlery, cutching and digging down tents. One Riding horse of 221 Company strayed.	
	2/6/18	9-30 a.m.	The Commanding Officer and Veterinary Officer inspected animals to decide which to be retained for Battalion Transport and which to be returned to Remounts Depot. Checking of Saddlery, vide Mobilization Tables. 9-20 a.m.	
		6-30 p.m.	Voluntary Church parade for R.C's 6-30 p.m. Voluntary Service for C. of E's. Lieut. Pascoe 264 Company proceeded to XIX CORPS GAS SCHOOL, NOUVION to undergo a course of instruction in Gas defence Measures.	
	3/6/18		The Commanding Officer and the Veterinary Officer's inspection of animals as on 2nd inst. Transport Personnel underwent Gas Tests. Checking of Saddlery as on 2nd inst.	
	4/6/18		All Transport of the Five Companies surplus to the establishment of a Machine Gun Battalion returned to advanced Transport Depot, ABBEVILLE. Work Exchanging of damaged L.G.S. Wagons and unserviceable Saddlery. 272 Company took over in exchange all damaged L.G.S. Wagons and unserviceable Saddlery of the Four Companies. Cleaning of Saddlery, cutching and digging down of tents continued. COLONEL. N. CHARTERIS A.M.G.O. visited camp. Court of Enquiry assembles to investigate the circumstances under which one Riding Horse strayed from the Horse lines on 1st JUNE and to fix the responsibility if any. PRESIDENT. CAPTAIN W.J. FAWKES. M.C. MEMBERS. LIEUT. N.W. WHIFFIN. LIEUT. F.G.T. WOODHEAD.	
	5/6/18		Work in Camp continued, animals distributed into small groups as instructed by XIX Corps, as a protection against Air Raids. 4 A.S.C. Drivers attached to Battalion for duty.	
	6/6/18		Transport Personnel of 272 Company distributed as reinforcements to other Companies. Animals inspected by A.D.V.S. Work in Camp continued.	
	7/6/18.		Inspection of harness by Commanding Officer. Work in camp continued.	
	8/6/18.		Camp visited by the I.M.G.U. 4th ARMY and the D.D.M.S. Work in Camp continued.	
	9/6/18.	11-30 a.m.	221, 262, and 264 Companies arrived. LIEUT. PASCOE rejoined from CORPS GAS SCHOOL NOUVION. Captain and Qmr. T.C. PIERCE. M.C. proceeded to the M.G.C. Base Depot. Work in Camp continued.	
	10/6/18.	9-15am	The Commanding Officer inspected the BATTALION. Rain prevented most parades.	
	11/6/18.	"	LIEUT. PASCOE was appointed GAS OFFICER and a course commenced under him. 2/Lieut. Billington was appointed PHYSICAL TRAINING OFFICER and a course commenced under him. These courses were of a weeks duration. LIEUT. GREENWELL was appointed ASSISTANT ADJUTANT. The Commanding Officer inspected the Battalion 9-15 a.m. Work continued in Camp.	
	12/6/18	"	The Commanding Officer inspected the Battalion at 9-15 a.m.	

A7092). Wt. W12839/M1293. 750,000. 1/17. D. D & L., Ltd. Forms/C2118/14.

Army Form C. 2118.

Instructions regarding War Diaries and Intelligence Summaries are contained in F. S. Regs., Part II. and the Staff Manual respectively. Title pages will be prepared in manuscript.

WAR DIARY
or
INTELLIGENCE SUMMARY.

(*Erase heading not required.*)

Place	Date	Hour	Summary of Events and Information	Remarks and references to Appendices
PONT REMY.	13/6/18	10 a.m.	COLONEL GORDON GILMOUR D.S.O. commandant XIX Corps Troops inspected the Battalion. Work in Camp continued.	
	14/6/18	12 noon	MAJOR BURN-CALLENDER INSPECTOR Physical Training and Bayonet Fighting, 4th ARMY lectured the Battalion, and the Officers at 2 p.m. COLONEL CHARTERIS D.S.O. D.I.M.G.U. visited the Battalion CAPTAIN DICK. R.A.M.C. arrived for duty.	
	15/6/18.		Work in Camp continued.	
	16/6/18.	11 a.m.	Battalion parade C.of E. for open air service . R.C's 9 a.m. at PONT REMY CHURCH. GERMAN aeroplanes flew over camp towards ABBEVILLE and returned at 11-30 p.m. No damage done to Camp.	
	17/6/18.	2 a.m.	GERMAN AEROPLANES flew over camp, no damage to camp, a few bombs dropped about two miles from camp. Major Dent. D.S.O. G.S.O. XIX Corps lectured the Officers on "Intelligence"	
	18/6/18	9 a.m.	The Commanding Officer inspected the Battalion. Eleven Officers attended one days lecture at School of Cookery 4th ARMY. Work carried on in camp.	
	19/6/18	"	Battalion Route March. Lecture by Captain Sandon Intelligence Officer XIX Corps on "The German Army"	
	20/6/18.	"	COLONEL CHARTERIS, D.S.O. D.I.M.G.U. inspected the Battalion and congratulated it onits turn out. In the afternoon COLONEL CHARTERIS lectured to the Battalion on "Common Sense" Battalion inter-Company Cross Country Run, Won by one Point by "A" Company, "B" Company second. In the evening the Commandant XIX Corps SChools lectured the Officers on "The Personnel of an Infantry Battalion in France at the present time"	
	21/6/18	"	Battalion Drill. In the afternoon the Battalion Shooting Team put up a very good performance against a crack Team of Marksmen from the Instructors of the V ARMY MUSKETRY SCHOOL, but they were eventually beaten by 85 Points. Score - Musketry Staff. 1622. "A" Battalion 1539 Points. 271 and 272 Companies arrive in camp, 272 Company divided up amongst the other four Companies	
	22/6/18	6-30 p.m.	Battalion Transport started on its march to Wood S.W. of QUERRIEU at point H 19 central Reference sheet 62 D, stopping for the night at BELLOY SUR SOMME. In the evening Major Dent D.S.O. lectured to the Officers on "The Tactics of the German Army"	See A Bn order No 4. d/-22/6/18 attached.
WOOD S.W. OF QUERRIEU.	23/6/18		In accordance with "A" Battalion M.G.C. Order No. 5 dated 22/6/18. the Battalion proceeded by train to POULAINVILLE, and from there marched to the 2ood S.W. of QUERRIEU to a point H 19 central. Reference Sheet 62 D.	See A Bn order No 5. d/-22/6/18 attached
	24/6/18.	9 a.m.	The Battalion dug shelters in the Wood S.W. of QUERRIEU.	

A7092). Wt. W12839/M1293. 750,000. 1/17. D. D & L., Ltd. Forms/C2118/14.

Army Form C. 2118.

WAR DIARY
or
INTELLIGENCE SUMMARY.
(*Erase heading not required.*)

Instructions regarding War Diaries and Intelligence Summaries are contained in F. S. Regs., Part II. and the Staff Manual respectively. Title pages will be prepared in manuscript.

Place	Date	Hour	Summary of Events and Information	Remarks and references to Appendices
WOOD S.W. OF QUERRIEU	25/6/18	9 a.m.	Battalion Drill. The Commanding Officer, 2nd in Command, O.C. Coys and two Section Commanders from each Company reconnoitred the line occupied by the 34th Machine Gun Battalion prior to relieving them on the morrow. Advance Party of American M.G. Battalion arrived to take over the Battalion Camp.	
BEAUCOURT.	26/6/18	6p.m.	The Battalion marched to BEAUCOURT and went into billets there. They were relieved at Wood S.W. QUERRIEU by 122nd American Machine Gun Battalion* *The destination of the Battalion was changed from VADENCOURT to BEAUCOURT. The Battalion did not relieve the 34th Battalion as stated in "A" M.G. Battalion Orders No 6. but sent guards to take over and guard the stores in the trenches occupied by the 34th Battn Machine Gun Corps.	See A Bn order No.6 d/-25/6/18 attached.
VILLERS-BOCAGE.	27/6/18.		The trenches, emplacements, stores etc which the Battalion was guarding, were taken over by the 2nd Life Guards Battalion Machine Gun Regt, in accordance with "A" M.G. Battalion order No. 7. In the evening in accordance with "A" M.G. Battn Order No. 9 dated 27/6/18 the Battalion marched into billets in VILLERS-BOCAGE.	See A Bn order No 7 d/-26/6/18 attached. See A Bn. order No.9 d/-27/6/18. attached.
	28/6/18.		The Battalion spent the morning cleaning up for the Commanding Officers inspection in the afternoon.	
EPERLECQUES.	29/6/18.		In accordance with "A" Battalion M.G. Order No. 10. the Battalion marched from VILLERS-BOCAGE to POULAINVILLE, and there entrained in two trains for AUDRUICQ, Battalion H.Q's, "A" & "B" Companies going on first train, "C" & "D" Companies on second train. The Battalion travelled all night.	
	30/6/18.	5 a.m.	The Battalion detrained at AUDRUICQ and marched into billets at EPERLECQUES.	

[signature]
Lieut. Col.
Commanding 30th Battalion Machine Gun Corps.

A7092). Wt. W12839/M1293 750,000. 1/17. D. D & L., Ltd. Forms/C2118/14.

SECRET COPY No. 11

'A' Battalion Machine Gun Corps Order No. 4.

Reference Maps. ABBEVILLE 14. LENS 11. & AMIENS 17.

22nd. June, 1918

1. In accordance with orders from XIX. Corps, 'A' Battalion Machine Gun Corps will be transferred by road and rail on the 22nd. and 23rd. June, from XIX. Corps to Australian Corps.

2. On arrival Battalion will be accommodated in wood South-west of QUERRIEU and will be administered by the Australian Corps.

3. The personnel and a proportion of Transport will move by rail on June, 23rd. under orders which will be issued later.

4. (a) The remainder of the Transport will move by road today June, 22nd. to BELLOY SUR SOMME. No restrictions as to route.

(b) The move of this Transport on the 23rd. will be under orders of the Australian Corps, which will be sent C/O Area Commandant, BELLOY SUR SOMME.

5. The Battalion Transport will move today, less the following vehicles:-

Vehicles.	Animals.
2 G. S. Wagons.	4 H. D
3 Field Kitchens	6 H. D.
1 Battalion Headquarter Limber	2 L. D.
4 Company Headquarter Limbers	8 L. D.
1 Mess Cart	1 L. D.
2 Water Carts	4 L. D.
2 G. S. Limbered Wagons	4 L. D.
	21 Riders.
15 Vehicles.	50 Animals.

This Transport will move by rail with the personnel on the 23rd. instant.

6. 'A' Coys. Field Kitchen will accompany the Transport by road. O. C. 'A' Coy will arrange to share Kitchens of 'B' & 'C' Coys. to cook for his Company.

7. Advance Party. The Battalion Transport Officer will detail an advance party of 1 N.C.O. per Coy to precede the column under 2nd. Lieut. G. C. Grimshaw. This party should leave as early as possible and report to Area Commandant, BELLOY SUR SOMME for billets.

8. The Quartermaster will issue rations and forage for the road party forthwith.

9. 'A' & 'C' Coys. will provide the 2 L.G.S.Wagons ~~to~~ mentioned para. 5 to travel by rail. These will be at the disposal of the Quartermaster.

10. Dinners for road party will be at 11 a.m. and party will leave camp at 1 p.m.

11. Each Coy. will detail 12 brakesmen per Coy. to move with Transport today. The Quartermaster will arrange to divert their rations. These men must be fit to do a heavy march they will have dinner early and report to Coy. Transport Officers at 12-30 p.m.

12. Coys. will arrange that they dispatch all stores and kit to day accept that which they can carry on their Headquarter Limber.

13. The Battalion Transport officer will send forward a party as early as possible on the 23rd. to the destination of the Battalion to arrange tentage and lines.

14. The Battalion Transport Officer will detail an orderly to remain at Office of Area Commandant, BELLOY SUR SOMME to receive any orders which may come for him.

15. Lieut. Parkin will travel with the rail party and will be in charge of the Transport.

16. The Quartermaster will arrange to return all furniture on loan to the Battalion today.

17. ACKNOWLEDGE.

G. Stewart Lt for Captain for
Lieut. Col.
Commanding 'A' Battalion Machine Gun Corps.

Issued by D. R. at a.m.

Copy No. 1 Commanding Officer
2 Quartermaster
3 Signal Officer
4 Transport Officer
5 O. C. 'A' Coy.
6 'B' "
7 'C' "
8 'D' "
9 H. Q. XIX. Corps.
10. Commandant Corps Troops.
11. War Diary.
12. do
13. File.
14. Australian Corps.

SECRET.

War Diary

"A" BATTALION MACHINE GUN CORPS ORDER No. 5. Copy No. 13

Reference Sheet. ABBEVILLE. 14.
LENS. 11.
AMIENS. 17.

22/6/18.

1. In continuation of "A" Battalion M.G. Corps order No. 4 of to-day, the Battalion and the remainder of the Transport will proceed by train to POULAINVILLE, leaving PONT REMY Station at 2 p.m. Sunday 23rd inst.

2. The Transport under Lieut. T.H. Parkin will move off at 10 a.m. to proceed to the station.

3. A loading party of 60 N.C.O's and men will be detailed by the O.C. "B" Coy to load Transport and stores, and to unload same at detraining station. Lieut. Dempster will be in charge of the party which will move off with the Transport. This Officer will obtain an entraining state from the Orderly Room and will report to R.T.O. at PONT REMY at 11 a.m.

4. The Battalion will parade at 11-45 a.m. on the Battalion Parade ground. Dress. Full Marching Order.

5. Order of March and entraining. Battn H.Q. "A" Coy, "B" Coy, "C" Coy, "D" Coy.

6. All Officers valises must be stacked at the Q.M. Stores by 9 a.m.

7. Remaining Stores of Companies must be loaded on their Headquarter Limber by 9-30 a.m.

8. Rations. (a) The unconsumed portion for the 23rd will be issued to the men
(b) For the 24th, rations will be delivered in bulk at the station, for the whole Battalion.

9. A Marching out state will be rendered by Company Commanders and Lieut. Parkin for the Transport. to the Orderly Room by 9-30 a.m.

10. A certificate that their portion of the camp and Transport Lines is clean will be handed in by O.C. Coys by 11-30 a.m. All personnel and kits must be clear of tents by 11 a.m. to allow Company Commanders to make a thorough inspection.

11 Routine.

Reveille	6 a.m.
Breakfast.	7 a.m.
Dinner.	11 a.m.
Tea	en route.

12. O.C. "C" Coy will provide a party of one N.C.O. and 15 men to report to the Q.M. Stores at 9 a.m. to ~~the~~ load the valises and stores on lorries.

13. Acknowledge.

Issued by D.R. at 7.45 p.m.

Captain for
Lieut. Col.
Commanding "A" Battalion Machine Gun Corps.

Copy No. 1. Commanding Officer.
2. Quartermaster.
3. Signal Officer.
4. "A" Company.
5. "B" "
6. "C" "
7. "D" "
8. Lieut. Parkin.

Copy No. 9. XIX Corps.
10 Commandant Corps Troops.
11. Australian Corps.
12.) War Diary.
13.) War Diary. ✓
14. File
15. R.S.M.

File

SECRET.

Reference Sheet.
62.D 1/40,000
57.D 1/40

'A' Battalion Machine Gun Corps Orders No. 6.

Copy.No. 18

25th. June, 1918.

1. 'A' Battalion Machine Gun Corps will relieve the 34th. Battalion Machine Gun Corps tomorrow, 26th. instant, in the 111. Corps area, Relief to be complete by evening.

2. 'A' Coy. will parade at 9 a.m. and move off independently with all its Transport, to the point where guides will be met, as arranged by O. C. Coy. direct with O. C. 'C' Coy. 34th. Battalion Machine Gun Corps Company Headquarters will be at C 11 b 9. 8.

3. Battalion Headquarter personnel with Headquarter Transport and B, C, & D Coys with their HeadquarterLimber and Fighting Limbers & Field Kitchens, will move off at 11 a.m. in that order. Distances of
100 x between each unit and its transport
150 x between each unit, and
25 x between each 2 vehicles, will be maintained throughout. Coys will provide their own brakesmen.

4. Route. For Battalion Headquarters B, C, D, Coys.:- QUERRIEU - FRECHENCOURT - MONTIGNY - BEAUCOURT - CONTAY - VADENCOURT.

5. Battalion Headquarters will be at Billet No. 7 VADENCOURT.
'B' Coy. will relieve 'B'34th. Battn. Machine Gun Corps. Coy H.Q. at V 20 d 4. 5.
'C' Coy. will relieve 'A' Coy. 34th. Battn. Machine Gun Corps. Coy. H.Q. at U 30 a 9. 1.
'D' Coy. will relieve 'D' Coy. 34th. Battn. Machine Gun Corps. Coy. H.Q. at U 28 c 7. 1.
Arrangements for relief have been made direct by O. C. Coys. concerned.

6. On arrival at new Battalion Headquarters 'B' Coy. will proceed at once to its position. The remaining Coys. will be met by guides and will proceed to their positions at 3 p.m.

7. As soon as relief is complete Coys, will send a cyclist orderly to Battalion Headquarters to report and to remain there. Map reference of Coy. H. Q. will be given and those of the gun positions within the first 24 hours after relief.

INSTRUCTIONS.

8. 'B' Coy. will provide the same working parties as have been provided by 'B' Coy. 34th. Battalion Mchine Gun Corps for the 18th. Battalion Machine Gun Corps.

9. Coys. will keep a strict guard on their animals whilst in this area.

10. 5 Signallers will be attached to each of A, B, & C Coys and 4 to D. Coy.

11. The Signalling Officer and two Officers per Coy. will go ahead to take over.

12. Coys. will submit a daily Situation Report and a daily Casualty Report to reach Battalion Headquarters by 2 p.m. daily. The Casualty Report will be from 12 noon to 12 noon.

13. Dress. Battle Order. Greatcoats worn Bandolier fashion and Mess Tins carried on Haversacks. Water Bottles to be filled. Steel Helmets to be carried on shoulder.

14. Rations for consumption up to the 26th. instant inclusive to be carried by Company arrangements. Rations for consumption on the 27th. will be drawn from POULAINVILLE tomorrow 26th.instant.

15. Blankets Will be rolled and carried by Companies on their Fighting Limbers also Valises. Packs will be stacked by Compnies at the Quartermaster Stores by 8 a.m. for conveyance by lorry to the new Battalion Transport lines. Each Company to provide two men to load these. All packs to be clearly marked with the owners Number, Name and Company.

16. ACKNOWLEDGE.

Captain for
Lieut. Col.
Commanding 'A' Battalion Machine Gun Corps.

Issued by D. R. at 9.45 p.m.

Copy No. 1 Commanding Officer.
2 Second in Command.
3 Battalion Transport Officer
4 Quartermaster.
5 Signalling Officer.
6 Intelligence Officer.
7. O. C. 'A' Coy.
8 do 'B' do
9 do 'C' do
10. do 'D' do
11 Medical Officer
12 Australian Corps
13 111. Corps.
14 34th. Battalion Machine Gun Corps.
15 18th. Division.
16. 58th. do
17 War Diary
18 do
19 R. S. M.
20 Spare
21. File.

SECRET. Copy No. 14

'A' Battalion Machine Gun/Order No. 7. (Corps inserted above: "Gun Corps/Order")

Reference Sheet 57 D. 2[illegible]th. June, 1918.

1. 'A' Battalion Machine Gun Corps is at BEAUCOURT in Corps Reserve, and will man Sectors as follows on the receipt of orders to move from 111. Corps:-

'A' Coy. will man the BAIZIEUX System on the Right Corps Front and will then come under the orders of the 58th. Division.

'B' Coy. will man the HENINCOURT - LAVIEVILLE Line, and will then come underthe orders of the 18th. Division.

'C' Coy. will man the BAIZIEUX System on theLeft Corps Front and will then come under the orders of the 18th. Division.

'D' Coy. will move to U 28 d 1. 1. andremain in Corps Reserve.

Battalion Headquarters is at Billet No. 11 BEAUCOURT.

2. Reconnaissance. (a) O. C. 'B' Coy. will be at 2nd. Life Guards Machine Gun Battalion Headquarters VADENCOURT at 9-30 a.m. with two Section Officers, all to be mounted, to meet the Commanding Officer and Officers of the 2nd. Life Guards Machine Gun Battalion and will conduct them round the HENINCOURT - LAVIEVILLE LINE. O. C. 'B' Coy. will ensure that he and his Section Officers are provided with Maps showing all the Gun Positions of his Sector.

(b) O. C. 'A' & 'C' Coys. each with two Section Officers will be at 2nd. Life Guards Machine Gun Battalion Headquarters at 2-30 p.m., all mounted, to meet Officer Commanding the 2nd. Life Guards Machine Gun Battalion and Officers, and will conduct them round the Sectors held by 'A' & 'C' Coys. O. C's. 'A' & 'C' Coys. will ensure that they and their Section Officers havethe necessary Maps.

(c) O. C. 'D' Coy. will conduct a Company Commander of the 2nd. Life Guard Machine Gun Battalion to the bivouacs at the disposal of his Company.

3. Parties in the Line. Guards of 1 Officer and 20 N.C.O's and men per Company are occupying the Company and Section Headquarters and the Gun positions, to ensure that all Maps, Stores, S. A. A., A. P., Tentage etc., will be preserved as taken over from the 54th. Battalion Machine Gun Corps, and the positions will be handed over correctlyand in a clean condition on Relief. These guards will remain at the position until relieved.

4. ACKNOWLEDGE.

W. J. Lawkins

Captain for Lieut. Col.

Commanding 'A' Battalion Machine Gun Corps.

Issued by D. R. at p.m.

Copy No. 1 Commanding Officer
2 Second in Command.
3 Signal Officer
4 ~~Intelligence~~ Officer.
5 Quartermaster.
6 Battalion Transport Officer.
7 ~~O. C.~~ 'A' Coy.
8 do 'B' do
9 do 'C' do
10. do 'D' do
11. 2nd. Life Guards Machine Gun Battalion.
12. 111. Corps.
13. ~~War Diary~~.
14. do
15. File.
16. Spare.
17. 58 Division
18. 18 do

SECRET. Copy No. 15

'A' Battalion Machine Gun Corps Order No. 9.

27th. June, 1918.

1. In continuation of 'A' Battalion Machine Gun Corps order No. 8 of today, the Battalion will not move at the time arranged.

2. The Battalion must be prepared to move at half an hours notice this afternoon. All men must remain in the vicinity of their billets with equipment ready. The Transport must stand to, but not hooked in.

3. On the order to parade being given Coys. will fall in, in front of their billets and will be joined by their Transport on passing the Transport Lines.

4. ROUTE. MOLLIENS au BOIS - VILLERS BOCAGE.

5. ORDER OF MARCH. Battalion Headquarters, 'A' Coy, 'B' Coy, 'C' Coy 'D' Coy, each with its own Transport. Battalion Headquarters will move off at Zero (which will be given) and Companies at minute intervals afterwards. Strict march discipline will be observed.

6. Billeting parties have gone ahead and Companies will be guided to billets on arrival.

7. GARRISONS IN THE LINE. These will remain in position until their sector is taken over by the 2nd. Life Guards Battalion Machine Gun Regiment when they will withdraw as follows:-

(a) Parties of 'B' & 'D' Coys. and guard at Transport Lines on relief will withdraw today to BEAUCOURT. Company Commanders will arrange to leave an N. C. O. to meet these parties and to conduct them to billets for the night. Breakfast ration for this party must be left behind. Companies will send necessary Transport tomorrow 28th. instant, to carry kits of these men, also a guide to bring them on to VILLERS - BOCAGE, which they must reach by 12 noon. O. C. 'B' Coy. will instruct the Officer with his line party to take chargeof the party of 'D' Coy.

(b) Parties of 'A' & 'C' Coy. will on relief tomorrow withdraw direct to VILLERS - BOCAGE. Companies to provide necessary Transport and guides.

8. ACKNOWLEDGE.

[signature]

Captain for
Lieut. Col.
Commanding 'A' Battalion Machine Gun Corps.

Issued by D. R. at p.m.

Copy No. 1	Commanding Officer.	11.	2nd. Life Guards M. G. Regt.
2	Second in Command.	12.	~~III. Corps.~~ RSM
3	Signal Officer	13.	War Diary.
4	Intelligence Officer	14.	do
5	Quartermaster.	15.	File
6.	Battalion Transport Officer		
7	O. C. 'A' Coy.	16.	Spare
8	do 'B' do	17.	58th. Division
9	do 'C' do	18.	18th.Division.
10	do 'D' do		

Original   Confidential

VR 5

War Diary

of

30th Battalion Machine Gun Corps

For the month of July 1918

Volume III   1-31 July 1918.

Instructions regarding War Diaries and Intelligence Summaries are contained in F. S. Regs., Part II. and the Staff Manual respectively. Title pages will be prepared in manuscript.

WAR DIARY
or
INTELLIGENCE SUMMARY.
(Erase heading not required.)

Army Form C. 2118.

Place	Date	Hour	Summary of Events and Information	Remarks and references to Appendices
EPERLECQUES	1/7/18.		Battalion Parade. The Regimental Sergeant Major took the Officers & N.C.O's of the Battalion in Close Order Drill.	
	2/7/18.		The Battalion fired Musketry & Machine Gun Practices. The Commanding Officer, Officers Commanding Companies & available Section Officers reconnoitred the ground around NORTHLEULINGHAM with a view to carrying out a defensive scheme by the Battalion to-morrow.	
	3/7/18	10 a.m.	The Battalion was inspected in a Defensive Scheme by the G.O.C. 30th Division, Major General Williams, C.M.G., D.S.O. on the training area.	
	4/7/18		B, C, & D Companies marched under Company arrangements to the Training Area & Carried out training under Company Commanders arrangements.	
		6p.m.	The Divisional Gas Officer lectured the Officers on "Protection against Gas".	
	5/7/18.		The Battalion spent the day cleaning up for the G.O.C's inspection on the morrow. The first trial of the Battalion Football Team took place in the evening.	
	6/7/18.		The Battalion was inspected by the Divisional General, Major General Williams C.M.G., D.S.O. The General remarked on excellent turnout of the Battalion and was especially pleased with the smartness of the Transport. In the evening the Battalion Football Team played a trial match against a team captained by Lieut. Wheatley.	
	7/7/18.		Church Parade at Divisional Headquarters. 2nd Lieut. H.J. Saqui reported to 90th Brigade at 8 a.m. to proceed with the Brigade Billeting Party.	
ST.MOMELIN	8/7/18		In accordance with 30th M.G.Bn. Order No. 11. the Battalion (less "C" Coy) marched to HAVERSHERGUE FARM near ST. MOMELIN where they stayed the night. C Coy marched under 90th Bde orders to RENESCURE.	Appendix 1.
Near TERDEGHEM.	9/7/18.		In accordance with 30th M.G.Bn. order No. 12 the Battalion (less "C" Coy) proceeded to NOORDPEENE where they stayed till 8-30 p.m. At 8-30 p.m. the Battalion continued its march, arriving at a point two miles S. of TERDEGHEM at 3-0a.m. 9th inst. where they bivouaced the rest of the night. C Coy moved by march route to EECKE under 90th Brigade Orders.	Appendix 2.
	10/7/18.		Companies moved off independently to billets which had been found for them in the morning "B" Coy Section Officers reconnoitred their portion of the Army (BERTHEN) Line.	
	11/7/18.		The Commanding Officer finally settled on C Coys gun positions in the Army (BERTHEN) Line. The Officers of "B" Coy made a reconnaissance of its portion of the line. "C" Coy manned the trenches & remained there throughout the night. The remaining Companies carried on with Company training.	
	12/7/18.		The G.O.C. inspected the positions of "C" Coy & half those of B Coy's in the Army Line Coys carried on with Coy Training. In the evening "B" Coy marched to their portion of the line and manned their positions during the night.	

(A7092). Wt. W12839/M1293. 750,000. 1/17. D. D. & L., Ltd. Forms/C.2118/14.

Instructions regarding War Diaries and Intelligence Summaries are contained in F. S. Regs., Part II. and the Staff Manual respectively. Title pages will be prepared in manuscript.

WAR DIARY
or
INTELLIGENCE SUMMARY.
(Erase heading not required.)

Army Form C. 2118.

Place	Date	Hour	Summary of Events and Information	Remarks and references to Appendices
Near TERDEGHEM.	13/7/18.		"B" Company marched back from the line . The remaining Coys carried on with Coy Training.	
	14/7/18.		Church of England Parade on D Coy's Parade Ground. Officers of B Coy completed their reconnaissance of positions in the line	see Appendix 3.
	15/7/18.		B. & C Coys moved to positions in rear of the line which they were to occupy in the event of an enemy attack. A. & D. Coys carried on with Coy training under Company Commanders.	
	16/7/18.		A. & D Coys at Company Commanders disposal. In the evening a concert was given to the Battalion by the 30th Divisional Concert Party.	
	17/7/18.		A Coy took over B. & C. Coys positions in the ARMY (BERTHEN) Line. B. & C. Coys were attached to the 89th & 21st Brigades respectively. Orders came through to assemble at Battle Stations at 3-30 a.m. next morning.	Appendix 4.
	18/7/18.		The Battalion assembled at Battle Stations & were in position by 4 a.m. B Coy acted under orders from the 89th Brigade, C Coy under orders from the 21st Brigade, & D Coy moved to assembly positions under orders from the 90th Brigade. The Battalion withdrew from Battle Stations at 6 a.m. General instructions as to the principles upon which Machine Guns should be utilised were issued to all concerned.	Appendix 5. See SG/32 d/- 18/7/18.
	19/7/18.		The Commanding Officer met the Officers Commanding A, B, & C Coys at C Coys Headquarters and held a conference there. "Test Orders" came through from Division.	
	20/7/18.		The Second-in-Command reconnoitred behind the left portion of the ARMY Line with a view to siting M.G. positions on a rear line of defence.	
	21/7/18.		The Commanding Officer met the Officers Commanding A, B, & C Coys at B. Coys Headquarters & held a conference. Church Parade for D Company.	
	22/7/18.		Five Officers & four N.C.O's of D Coy reconnoitred the BERTHEN Line. Rest of Coys carried on with Company Training. "Test Orders" sent through 12 noon from Division.	
	23/7/18.		A Company improved emplacements in the Army Line & carried on with Company Training . Officers of C. & D. Coys made a reconnaissance of BERTHEN Line. Coy Training by C. & D. Coys.	
	24/7/18.		Lieut. P.S. Greenwell rejoined from Hospital & took over duties of Assistant Adjutant.	
	25/7/18.		Officers and N.C.O's of B. & C. Coy's reconnoitred the ARMY Line. Training continued by other Companies.	
	26/7/18.		Company Training by B. C. & D. Coys. Section Officers of B. Coy reconnoitred the ARMY Line. The Commanding Officer reconnoitred ARMY Line with Corps Machine Gun Officer. Second-in-Command accompanied C.O. of E. Machine Gun Bn. round the Line. Officers of D. Coy reconnoitred ARMY Line.	

(A7092). Wt. W12839/M1293. 750,000. 1/17. D. D. & L., Ltd. Forms/C.2118/14.

Instructions regarding War Diaries and Intelligence Summaries are contained in F. S. Regs., Part II. and the Staff Manual respectively. Title pages will be prepared in manuscript.

WAR DIARY
or
INTELLIGENCE SUMMARY.
(Erase heading not required.)

Army Form C. 2118.

Place	Date	Hour	Summary of Events and Information	Remarks and references to Appendices
Near TERDEGHEM.	27/7/18.		Companies carried on with Coy Training. B. Coy Section Officers reconnoitred Army Line. Captain Tresham, Captain Swanston & Lieut. Wheatley attended a M.G. demonstration at CAMIERS.	
	28/7/18.		The Commanding Officer reconnoitred the sites of Battery Positions near MONT ROUGE. Coy's carried on with Company Training.	
	29/7/18.		Officers of C. & D. Coy's reconnoitred Army Line. Company Training continued.	
	30/7/18.		Officers of C. & D. Coy's reconnoitred Army Line. Commanding Officer visited C. Coy. A Coy carried on with improving positions in the Army Line.	
	31/7/18.		A Company still manning positions in the ARMY Line. B. & C. Coys carried on with Company Training during the day & sent up working parties to dig emplacements during the night. Six of B. Coys working party were wounded by shell fire whilst returning to billets. Sixty men of D. Company proceeded to join B. Coy & 60 to join C. Coy to be attached to these Coy's to take part in an operation.	

H.G. Roberts
Lieut. Colonel,
Commanding 30th Battalion Machine Gun Corps.

5th August, 1918.

(A7092). Wt. W12839/M1293. 750,000. 1/17. D. D. & L., Ltd. Forms/C.2118/14.

Confidential

Appendix

to

War Diary

of

30th Battalion Machine Gun Corps

For month of July 1918

Appendix III

1-31 July 1918.

Appendix!

SECRET. COPY No. 16

30th. Battalion Machine Gun Corps Order No. 11.

Reference Sheets.
HAZEBROUCK 5a 1/100,000.
Sheet 27 1/40,000.
Sheet 27a (Eastern Half) 1/40,000. 7th. July, 1918.

1. The 30th. Division (less Artillery) will move to the Xth. Corps area by march route on the 8th. 9th. and 10th. inst., and will relieve the 41st. French Division in Corps Reserve.

2. The 30th. Battalion Machine Gun Corps (less C Coy.) will move on the 8th. 9th. inst. under the orders for the 89th. Infantry Brigade Group.
STARTING POINT. Fork Roads 500x S. of the G in GANSPETTE.
Time of Starting 10 a.m.
ROUTE:- NORDBROUCK - CROME STRAETE - Fork Roads G 33 c

3. BILLETING. Billets will be provided in the HAVERSHERGUE FARM area (M 2 c & d)
Lieut. Dempster and billeting party of 1 N. C. O. of H. Q., A., B., & D. Coys. will meet 89th. Infantry Brigade represntative at Office of Area Commandant, St. MOMELIN at 10 a.m. This party will leave on cycles at 9-0 a.m., and meet the column on main road on arrival to guide Companies to billets.

4. C. Coy. 30th. Battalion Machine Gun Corps will move on the 8th. and 9th. inst. under orders issued for the 90th. Brigade Group, according to the following March Table:-

Serial Number.	Unit.	From.	To.	STARTING POINT Place.	Time.
3.	C Coy. 30th. Bn. Machine Gun Corps.	EPERLECQUES	REMESCURE Area.	Road Junction TILQUES. N. 19 c 2.7 (Sheet 27a Eastern Half)	9-45 a.m.

Route:- TILQUES - St. OMER - ARQUES.
Position in the March Column will be immediately in rear of Serial No. 2, 2/13th. Bn. (Queens Westminsters) London Regiment.
March Table for move on the 9th. inst. to St. SYLVESTRE - HECKE Area will be forwarded by 90th. Brigade Later, when O. C. Company will issue his own move orders.
A billeting party has proceeded today, and will guide the Company to billets on arrival.
Communication will be maintained between O. C. C. Coy. and Headquarters.
(a) During the move by D. R. L. S.
(b) On completion of the move by two orderlies being sent to Headquarters, one to remain, the other to return to the Company.
O. C. C Coy. will also report completion of each move to 90th. Brigade Headquarters by quoting the Serial Number and time of completion. Brigade Headquarters will be at REMESCURE for night 8/9th.

5. The 30th. Division while in Corps Reserve, will, in case of attack, be prepared on receipt of orders to man the [illegible] LINE.

In the event of orders being received, Companies will be attached to Brigades as follows:-

A Coy. in Divisional Reserve.
B Coy. to 89th. Infantry Brigade on the LEFT.
C Coy. to 90th. Infantry Brigade on the RIGHT.
D Coy. to 21st. Infantry Brigade in RESERVE.

6. RECONNAISSANCE. Orders for a preliminary reconnaissance have already been issued. All Officers and Senior N. C. O's must as soon as possible become thoroughly acquainted with the line and the positions they may be called upon to occupy.

Company Commanders will report forthwith to Brigade Commanders so that they may receive instructions in case orders are received to man the line.

7. COMMUNICATION. Companies must at all times keep the closest possible touch with Battalion Headquarters, so that orders may be issued to them without unnecessary delay.

8. MARCH DISCIPLINE. The following distances will be maintained on the march:-

Between	Battalions	500 yards
do	Companies	100 do
do	a unit and its Transport	100 yards
do	each units Transport if Brigaded	100 yards.

INSTRUCTIONS.

1. C. Coy. will move off independently to reach the Starting Point at time ordered, but will notify Headquarters when ready to move.

2. The Battalion (less C Coy.) will form up in the following order, ready to move at 9-40 a.m. and will march to the Starting Point via QUEST - MONT :-

Headquarters, A. Coy, B. Coy, D. Coy. Transport (in same order as Companies.)

Head of Column at Cross Roads K 27 c 4.2. (Sheet 27a Eastern Half)

3. DRESS. Marching Order, Water Bottles full, Steel Helmets worn.

4. BLANKETS. Rolled in bundles of 10, labelled and stacked at Quartermasters Stores by 6-30 a.m.

5. STORES. Companies will carry all stores, kits, &c. on their own limbers.

6. RATIONS & FORAGE. For 8th. instant will be carried by Companies on Field Kitchens and Limbers.

For 9th. inst., will be carried for C. Coy. on G. S. Wagon, and for remainder under Quartermasters arrangements.

7. LOADING PARTY. of 1 N. C. O. and 12 men will be detailed by O. C. B Coy. to report at Quartermasters Stores at 7-45 a.m.

8. CLEANLINESS OF BILLETS. Company Commanders will render a certificate to Orderly Room an hour before marching out that billets have been left clean.

9. Marching Out states will be handed in at the same time.

10. Slow moving parties will be detailed to march in rear of each column, with an Officer in charge, to bring along men who fall out.

11. ACKNOWLEDGE.

Captain for
Lieut. Col.

Commanding 30th. Battalion Machine Gun Corps.

Issued by D. R. at p.m.

Copy No. 1. Commanding Officer
2. Second in Command.
3. 89th. Infantry Brigade.
4. 90th. Infantry Brigade.
5. Battalion Transport Officer.
6. Quartermaster.
7. Intelligence Officer.
8. Signalling Officer.
9. O. C. A. Coy.
10. do B. do
11. do C. do
12. do D. do
13. 30th. Division.
14. R. S. M.
15. File.
16. War Diary.
17. do
18. Spare.

SECRET. COPY No. 14.

30th. Battalion Machine Gun Corps Order No. 14.

Reference Sheet 27 & 28. 14th. July, 1918.

1. The following moves will take place on the 15th. instant and will be completed by 6 p.m. on that date.

(a) 'C' Coy. 30th. Battalion Machine Gun Corps to Right Brigade Sector of Army Line on Divisional Front.

Company Headquarters in the vicinity of Q 17 c 9.8.

Transport in vicinity of Q 20 c 4.8

(b) 'B' Coy. 30th. Battalion Machine Gun Corps to Left Brigade Sector of the Army Line on the Divisional Front.

Company Headquarters in the vicinity of R 2 d 2.8.

Transport in vicinity of S 11 a 0.2

2. The following positions will be manned permanently

'C' Company:-

2 Guns in vicinity of Q 33 b 1.9.
2 Guns in vicinity of R 25 c 7.3
2 Guns in vicinity of R 19 d 7.3
2 Guns in vicinity of R 23 b 4.8

'B' Company:-

2 Guns in vicinity of R 21 a 3.2
2 Guns in vicinity of R 22 b 6.9
2 Guns in vicinity of R 17 c 5.6
2 Guns in vicinity of R 12 b 3.1

3. In the event of a heavy hostile bombardment opening, the remaining eight guns of each Company will move to the following positions:-

'C' Company:-

2 Guns to	R 25 c 7.3
2 Guns to	R 19 d 7.3
2 Guns to	R 26 b 3.8
2 Guns in reserve at	R 19 b 4.6

'B' Company:-

2 Guns to	R 18 c 2.3
2 Guns to	R 17 c 5.6
2 Guns to	R 17 b 7.1
2 Guns to	R 18 a 7.7

4. The O. C. 'C' Company will be Group Commander of the Defensive Machine Guns in the Right Brigade Sector, and will in the event of a battle, be with the G. O. C., Right Brigade.

The O. C. 'B' Company will be Group Commander of the Left Brigade Sector and will in the event of a battle, be with G. O. C., Left Brigade.

5. In the event of the order being received to Man Battle Stations, the Headquarters of the 30th. Battalion Machine Gun Corps will move to K 32 b 5.1

'A' Company will move to the vicinity of Q 17 c 9.8

'D' Company will move to the vicinity of R 2 d 2.8

The Officers Commanding 'A' & 'D' Companies will report to the G. O. C., Infantry Brigade of the Sector in which they are situated and to the Machine Gun Group Commander of that sector.

6. In the event of the Right Brigade making an immediate counter attack, two sections of 'A' Company will be detached to this Brigade for the purpose of consolidation. Similarly, should the Left Brigade make an immediate counter attack, two sections of 'D' Company will be detached to this Brigade for the same purpose.

The Officers Commanding 'A' & 'D' Companies and the Officers of the Sections thus detailed for detachment, will make the most careful reconnaissance of the Areas mentioned in the 30th. Divisional Defence Scheme, as the probable objectives.

The remaining Guns will be in Divisional Reserve, and will probably be used to reinforce the Machine Gun Defence of the Army Line and to assist the advance of our troops by covering barrage fire.

Each Group Commander will, with a view to the above, reconnoitre the positions from which the maximum supporting fire may be given to counter-attacks mentioned in 30th. Divisional Defence Scheme, and will have prepared positions on his front for an addition of 24 guns for the purpose of reinforcing the existing guns for covering fire. They will arrange for ammunition dumps in the vicinity of those positions.

8. ACKNOWLEDGE.

W J Laidlaw

Captain for
Lieut. Col.
Commanding 30th. Battalion Machine Gun Corps.

Issued by D. R. at 10:30 p.m.

Copy No. 1 Commanding Officer.
2 Second in Command.
3 Intelligence Officer.
4 Signal Officer.
5 Medical Officer
6 Quartermaster
7 O. C. 'A' Coy.
8 do 'B' do
9 do 'C' do
10 do 'D' do
11 30th. Division.
12 89th. Infantry Brigade.
13 90th. Infantry Brigade.
14 35th. Division.
15 33th. Division
16. R. S. M.
17 War Diary.
18 do
19 File.
20 Spare.

SECRET. COPY No.

30th Battalion Machine Gun Corps Order No. 15.

Reference Sheet 27. 17th July 1918.

1. "A" Company, 30th Battalion Machine Gun Corps will relieve the 8 Guns of "B" Company and the 8 Guns of "C" Company, permanently manning the Army Line, to-night 17th inst. Relief to be completed by 12 midnight.

O.C. "A" Company will establish his Headquarters with or near the Headquarters of "B" Company in R.3.c., and will establish his Transport Lines in the vicinity of Q.11.a.0.2. ("B" Companies Transport Lines)

2. After relief "B" Company will concentrate in the vicinity of R.2.d. and R.3.c. and will be attached to the 89th Infantry Brigade

"C" Company will concentrate in the vicinity of Q.17.d. and will be attached to the 21st Infantry Brigade.

Completions of relief will be notified by the code word "RATS"

ACKNOWLEDGE.

[signature]

Captain for
Lieut. Col.

Commanding 30th Battalion Machine Gun Corps.

Issued by D. R. at 1.35 p.m.

Copy No. 1. Commanding Officer.
2. Second in Command.
3. 30th Division.
4. 30th Division "Q"
5. 30th Division Train.
6. 89th Infantry Brigade.
7. 90th Infantry Brigade.
8. 21st Infantry Brigade.
9. O.C. "A" Company.
10. " "B" "
11. " "C" "
12. " "D" "
13. 35th Division.
14. 36th Division.

COPY No. 10

SECRET. 30th. Battalion Machine Gun Corps Order No. 16.

17th July 1918.

Reference Sheet 27 & 28 1/40, 000.
Berthen & Kemmel 1/10,000.

1. (a) In the event of a general bombardment opening or on the order "Assemble at Battle Stations", 'D' Coy. 30th. Battalion Machine Gun Corps will be attached to the 90th. Infantry Brigade and will move under orders to be issued by that Brigade to assembly positions in the Mt. COKEREELE defensive area and that country between BOESCHEPE - BERTHEN Road and the road running through R 11 central to R 13 central. Until receipt of further orders 'D' Coys. Headquarters will remain in present position at P 15 a 9.5.

(b) In the event of a general bombardment opening or on the order " Assemble at Battle Stations" 'B' Coy. 30th. Battalion Machine Gun Corps will be attached to 89th. Infantry Brigade and will move under orders to be issued by that Brigade to assembly positions VLENVICKHOVE and WESTEN MOLEN defensive areas, east of the Road from R 11 central - R 17 central. 'B' Company 30th. Battalion Machine Gun Corps will have Headquarters at R 3 c 2.3. and the personnel will be accommodated in the vicinity of these Headquarters.

(c) In the event of a general bombardment opening or on the order "Assemble at Battle Stations" 'C' Coy. 30th. Battalion Machine Gun Corps will be attached to 21st. Infantry Brigade and will move under orders to be issued by that Brigade, to Assembly positions in the GODEWAERSVELDE Area. 'C' Coy. 30th. Battalion Machine Gun Corps will have Headquarters at Q 17 d 8.1 and the personnel will be accommodated in the vicinity of these Headquarters.

The role of these Companies will be to support counter-attacks of the Brigades to which they are attached, under orders to be issued by the Brigade Commanders concerned.

BATTLE HEADQUARTERS.

Brigade Headquarters of both 89th. & 90th. Infatry Brigades will be established about R 2 d 2.8.

Brigade Headquarters of the 21st. Infatry Brigade will be notified later, but will probably be in the vicinity of Q 17 c 9.8.

Headquarters 30th. Battalion Machine Gun Corps will be with Divisional Headquarters at LESCISEAUX K 32 b.

2. On receipt of orders to occupy the Army Line, 'B' Coy. 30th. Battalion Machine Gun Corps will reinforce those guns of 'A' Coy. 30th. Battalion Machine Gun Corps which are in position in the localities LA MONTAGNE, Mt. KOKEREELE, VLENVICKHOVE, WESTENMOLEN, and O. C. 'B' Coy. will become Group Commander for all Machine Guns in these localities.

Similarly, 'C' Coy. 30th.Battalion Machine Gun Corps will reinforce the guns of 'A' Coy. 30th. Battalion Machine Gun Corps holding the COQ DE PAILLES and the MONT DES CATS localities, and O. C. ' C ' Coy. will become Group Commader for all Machine Guns in these localities.

'D' Coy. 30th. Battalion Machine Gun Corps will be in Divisional Reserve with 21st. Infatry Brigade, and will move to the area around GODEWAERSVELDE.

3. ACKNOWLEDGE.

W Hawke

Captain for
Lieut. Col.

Commading 30th. Battalion Machine Gun Corps.

Issued by S. D. R. at 1-35 p.m.

Distribution as for 30th. Battalion Machine Gun Corps Order No. 15.

SECRET.

Copy No 34

30 BATTALION, MACHINE GUN CORPS.

No. S.G./32

Date 18-7-18

As in the event of battle the success of operations must largely depend on the initiative of subordinate Machine Gun Commanders, the following general instructions as to the principles upon which Machine Guns should be utilized are issued for guidance and careful study.

A. THE ACTION OF MACHINE GUN SECTIONS CLOSELY SUPPORTING A COUNTER ATTACK.

Objects (a) The obtaining and maintenance of superiority of fire against enemy posts which are holding up our advance.

(b) The consolidation of all ground captured.

(1) The advance should be by sections i.e. the section of 4 guns should be the tactical Unit covering its own advance and under the control of its own Commander.

(2) The section should advance by bounds to and from positions, generally on the flanks from which the attack of the Infantry can be supported by direct overhead fire.

(3) In the advance as in the defence, sections should be disposed in depth as far as possible. They are especially responsible for the protection of the flanks of the counter attacking troops.

(4) Sections will advance in formation as closely resembling the formation of the Infantry as possible. They should be sufficiently in rear of the Infantry to prevent any possibility of their being involved in a melée but sufficiently close to ensure their being able to give adequate and direct support.

(5) Bounds should be made after reconnaissance. Such reconnaissance can be greatly assisted by the most careful previous study of the ground over which the counter attack is likely to take place.

Such preliminary reconnaissance of the ground by all ranks is of absolutely vital importance.

(6) Full use must be made of fighting limbers and pack animals which must be boldly pushed forward.

Otherwise it will be impossible for the ammunition supply to be maintained and the personnel will be unduly exhausted before they are actually engaged in the battle.

(7) The difficulty of Ammunition Supply can be largely minimised by the establishment of dumps of S.A.A. in well defined spots in the forward area known to all ranks.

(8) It must be most carefully impressed upon all gunners that promiscuous firing without a definite object is merely a waste of ammunition, and is liable to give away unnecessarily the position of their guns.

(9) The closest liaison with Infantry must be maintained at all times.

(10) On the capture of a position section commanders will so dispose their guns as to protect and hold the ground which has been won.

(11) Progress Reports must be forwarded to the Headquarters of the Machine Gun Company to which the section belongs. Such reports while not being unduly verbose should contain all information likely to be of value.

B. THE ACTION OF A MACHINE GUN COMPANY SUPPORTING THE COUNTER -ATTACK OF A NEIGHBOURING BRIGADE.

Object. The obtaining and maintenance of superiority of fire over the enemy by long range overhead fire.

(1). As it is not probable that much time would be available for preparation for the support of such a counter attack it is imperative that reconnaissance be made and positions selected from which long range covering fire could be given.
(2) Positions from which observation can be obtained should be selected.
(3) Sections should work as Batteries and bring concentrated fire to bear on enemy positions which appear to be holding up our advance.
(4) Sections must be prepared to move at short notice, as it is quite probable that they may be recalled to carry out another task.
(5) Reports as to the Progress of the Counter Attack should be forwarded to the Machine Gun Company Commander.

C. ACTION OF A MACHINE GUN COMPANY SENT FORWARD TO REINFORCE THE THE MACHINE GUN DEFENCE OF THE ARMY LINE.

(1). The Forward Machine Gun Defence of the Army Line will be completed. Map showing the defence has already been issued with details as to the posts which are already permanently manned.
(2) A Second Line of Machine Gun Defence will be reconnoitred and the remaining 8 guns of each Supporting Company will move to those positions to form a rear system of Machine Gun Defence. The O.C. of the Company occupying the Machine Gun Defences of the Army Line will reconnoitre those positions forthwith.

Lieut. Colonel,

18th July 1918. Commanding 30th Battalion Machine Gun Corps.

Original

aB ~~AB~~

Confidential

VR 6

War Diary

of

30th Battalion Machine Gun Corps

for the

Month of August 1918

Volume 4

1-31 August 1918

Instructions regarding War Diaries and Intelligence Summaries are contained in F. S. Regs., Part II. and the Staff Manual respectively. Title pages will be prepared in manuscript.

WAR DIARY
or
INTELLIGENCE SUMMARY.
(Erase heading not required.)

Army Form C. 2118.

Place	Date	Hour	Summary of Events and Information	Remarks and references to Appendices
Nr. TERDEGHEM	1/8/18.		"A" Company improved their positions in BERTHEN Line. "B" Company with 2 Sections of "D" Company attached, and "C" Company with 2 Sections of "D" Company attached proceeded to the battle positions near MT.ROUGE. Casualties. "B" Coy. 1 killed, "C" Coy 1 wounded, "D" Coy 1 wounded.	Order No. 18.
	2/8/18.		"B", "C", and "D" Companies dug themselves in in their battery positions. In the evening orders came from the 35th Machine Gun Battalion that the operation was postponed and "B", "C" and "D" Coys were withdrawn.	
	3/8/18.		Day spent in cleaning up guns and equipment etc.	
	4/8/18.		An Army Church Parade Service was held in the Hangar at Terdeghem in commemoration of the 4th Anniversary of the outbreak of War. G.O.C. Commanding Second Army (General Sir Herbert C.O. Plumer, G.C.B., G.C.M.G., G.C.V.O., A.D.C., was present	
	5/8/18.		During the night 5/6th skeleton teams of B. C. & D Coys proceeded to MT. ROUGE with a view to carrying out an operation.	Order No. 19.
	6/8/18.		All available ranks cheered H.M. the King as he passed on his way from STEENVOORDE to SAN SYLVESTRE CAPEL. Operation mentioned yesterday was cancelled and during the night 6/7th the skeleton teams were withdrawn to B & C. Coy's billets.	

(A9475) Wt W2358/P360 600,000 12/17 D. D. & L. Sch. 52a. Forms/C2118/15

Instructions regarding War Diaries and Intelligence Summaries are contained in F. S. Regs., Part II. and the Staff Manual respectively. Title pages will be prepared in manuscript.

WAR DIARY
or
INTELLIGENCE SUMMARY.
(Erase heading not required.)

Army Form C. 2118.

Place	Date	Hour	Summary of Events and Information	Remarks and references to Appendices
Nr. TERDEGHEM.	7/8/18.		"D" Company marched back to TERDEGHEM. "A" Company were relieved in the BERTHEN Line by a Coy of the 35th M.G. Battalion and occupied the Reserve Coys billet near LANCET FARM. Remaining Companies cleaned up after their night in the open.	Order No. 20
	8/8/18.		During the night "A" Company relieved a Company of the 35th M.G. Battalion in the left Sub-Sector of the line. They had two men killed and 5 men wounded. 4 Mules were also killed from A "B" Company held a Boxing Tournament. Remaining Coys carried on with Company training.	
	9/8/18.		"A" Company completed the relief of three guns which it had been impossible to relieve the night before.	
	10/8/18		"D" Company moved forward to forward Area and took over from the Reserve Company of 35th Bn M.G.C. their Headquarters at Farm near LANCET FARM. B & C Coys relieved Coys of 35th Bn. M.G.C. in the line. Lieut. A Walker of "A" Company was killed by shell Fire.	
	11/8/18.		1 Officer and 4 men of D Coy paraded for Army Church Parade & afterwards marched past the KING.	
	12/8/18.		1 O.R. "B" Coy killed by shell fire. Harassing fire (5,000 rounds) was carroed out through the night.	
	13/8/18.		1 O,R. "A" Company killed by shell fire. Harassing fire continued as yesterday. 1 Officer 50 O.R's were attached from Reception Camp 30th Division for working up the line.	
	14/8/18.		1 O.R. "D" Company wounded by shell fire, while on a working party. Harassing fire was carried out, about 6,000 rounds expended. Two Officers and 40 O.R's were attached from "F" Bn. M.G.C.	
	15/8/18.		1 O.R. wounded by shell fire. "D" Company from Reserve relieved "A" Company in the line.	Order No.21.
	16/8/18.		Lieut. Orchard was slightly wounded in the Knee by shell fire, 2 O.R!s "A" Company were gassed and 1 man of B Coy was wounded by shellfire. A combined harassing fire shoot was carried out with the Artillery.	
	17/18/8/18.		No casualties. Harassing fire 2000 rounds per Coy, and an extra 3000 fired owing to suspected relief opposite us. Major Leah, 35th Bn. M.G.C. arrived at LANCET FARM.	

(A9475) Wt W2358/P365 6,0,000 12/17 D. D. & L. Sch. 52a. Forms/C2118/15

Instructions regarding War Diaries and Intelligence Summaries are contained in F. S. Regs., Part II. and the Staff Manual respectively. Title pages will be prepared in manuscript.

WAR DIARY
or
INTELLIGENCE SUMMARY.
(Erase heading not required.)

Army Form C. 2118.

Place	Date	Hour	Summary of Events and Information	Remarks and references to Appendices
Nr.	18/8/18.		2 Officers & 6 O.R's of "F" Bn. M.G.C. left for their Battalion.	
TERDEGHEM.	19/8/18.		No. Casualties. 35th Bn. M.G.C. and "A" Coy 30th Bn. move into the line, to take up their positions.	Order No. 22.
MONTAIGNE QUARRY.	20/8/18.		All batteries reported ready by 9 p.m. "G" Branch of Bn. H.Q. move to Divisional Advanced H.Qrs.	
	21/8/18	2-5am	30th Division attacked and captured DRANOUTRE RIDGE. The heavy M.G. Barrage of 148 guns supported the attack. Guns of the 30th and 35th Division were under the Command of Lieut. Col. Roberts, M.C., while 12 guns of 41st Division and 16 guns of 36th Division co-operated. Operation entirely sucessful, about 150 being captured and all objectives taken. Infantry report M.G. Barrage very good and thick, no shorts. During barrage 1 O.R. wounded "C" Coy.	
		8-0am	Movement reported by 90th Bde. on new front, and counter preparation was fired on S.O.S. lines. During day 1 Gun team 5 O.R's wounded, no other casualties reported. Operation orders attached. Congratulatory messages received from Army and Divisional Commanders.	Order No. 23.
	22/8/18.		Counter preparation shoots were carried out at irregular intervals during night. M.G's responded to S.O.S. call at midnight and during early morning, though it appeared to be false alarms both times. Lieut. B.T. Holloway wounded by shell fire while visiting an O.P. 1 O.R. "A" Company wounded and one gassed.	
	23/8/18.		Battalion Rear Headquarters moved from ZION MILL TERDEGHEM to advanced Division LA MONTAGNE. Lieut. Whiffen "B" Coy wounded by shell fire also 2 O.R's of B Coy killed, 8 O.R's wounded. Major Parker took over Command of the Battalion as Col. Roberts, M.C. went on leave.	
	24/8/18.		Two O.R's "C" Coy wounded. "A" Coy's billet set on fire by shell fire, everything burnt except two fore-portions of the limbers, three guns, four tripods, and a few accessories. Companies carried out harassing fire as per programme.	
	25/8/18.		Carried out harassing fire as per programme.	
	26/8/18.		2nd Lieut. C. Stephens & 2nd Lieut. L.E. Lewis reported for duty with this Battalion. 2nd Lieut Stephens posted to "A" Company. 2nd Lieut. Lewis posted to "B" Company. Companies carried out harassing fire on enemy tracks, roads, and tender spots. Enemy shelled "B" Company night firing positions with Gas.	
	27/8/18.		"A" Company relieved "C" Company in Centre Group, there were no casualties. The two other Companies carried out harassing fire as per programme.	Order No. 24.

(A9175) Wt W2358/P360 600,000 12/17 D. D. & L. Sch. 52a. Forms/C2118/15

Instructions regarding War Diaries and Intelligence Summaries are contained in F. S. Regs., Part II. and the Staff Manual respectively. Title pages will be prepared in manuscript.

WAR DIARY
or
INTELLIGENCE SUMMARY.
(Erase heading not required.)

Army Form C. 2118.

Place	Date	Hour	Summary of Events and Information	Remarks and references to Appendices
MONTAGNE QUARRY.	28/8/18.		A very quiet day - usual harassing fire carried out at night.	
	29/8/18.		Activity on both sides below normal - about 22 large fires observed in enemy back areas all day and during the night - especially behind ARMENTIERES and BAILLEUL. Two terrific explosions heard at 2-20 a.m. and large columns of smoke and flame observed at bearing of 170° Grid of M.27.b.5.9. Two more explosions were heard at 3-5 a.m. & 3-40 a.m. direction not located but certainly in enemy lines.	
	30/8/18.		Messages were received all day to the effect that the enemy were retiring on our front. Patrols from our Division reporting from BAILLEUL Railway Station had not yet got into touch with the enemy. Lieut. Barrett. 2nd Lieuts. Clarke & Bishop reported for duty with the Battn. Lieut. Barrett was posted to "D" Company, 2nd Lieut. Clarke to "B" Company and 2nd Lieut. Bishop to "A" Company.	
	31/8/18.		Enemy still retiring on our front. Our Infantry established themselves East of NEUVE EGLISE. Patrols of Infantry working further Eastward met with no resistance. At 8-30 a.m. the Commanding Officer (Major O.M. Parker) attended a conference at 89th Brigade Headquarters as a result of which two sections from each of the following Companies A. B. & D. were lent to the three Brigades, and the remaining two Sections of each Company concentrated at WESTOUTRE. "C" Company was sent forward for duty with the advancing Infantry, and in marching to their destination, Major W.R. Lewis, Lieut. Trethowan and 2 O.R's were wounded and 1 O.R. killed. Major Parker remained at "B" Coy Headquarter which then became Forward Battalion Headquarters. Battalion Transport moved up from NONE BOSCH to WESTOUTRE.	

O.M. Parker
Major,
Commanding 30th Battalion Machine Gun Corps.

(A9175) Wt W2358/P360 600,000 12/17 D. D. & L. Sch 52a. Forms/C2118/15

AB

Appendix
of
War Diary
30 Battalion Machine Gun Corps.
For the Month of August 1918.

Volume 4

1/31 August.

SECRET.

ADDENDUM to 30th. Battalion Machine Gun Corps Order No. 18.

Advanced Headquarters of 30th Battalion Machine Gun Corps will open at the present Headquarters of "C" Company at Q.17.d.8.1. at 6 p.m. 1st August, and will open with Headquarters of 35th Battalion Machine Gun Corps (location of which has already been notified) at 6 p.m. August, 2nd.

Subsequent to the operations, at a time to be notified later, Advanced Headquarters will again reopen at Q.17.d.8.1. until the withdrawal of Companies from the line is complete.

W. J. Fawkes

Captain for
Lieut. Col.

Commanding 30th. Battalion Machine Gun Corps.

31st July 1918.

Copies to all recipients of 30th. Battalion Machine Gun Corps Order No. 18.

SECRET. Copy No. 17

30th Battalion Machine Gun Corps Order No. 18.

Reference Sheets 27. (1/40,000)
BAILLEUL 28. S.W. 3. 1/10,000
KEMMEL 28. S.W. 1. 1/10,000

30th July 1918.

1. At ZERO hour in the early morning of August 3rd, 1918, the 35th Division intend to attack and capture the DRANOUTRE Ridge.

2. The 30th Battalion Machine Gun Corps (less "A" Coy) has been attached to the 35th Division in order to take part in this operation.

3. The guns of B, C, and D Companies, 30th Bn. M.G. Corps will form part of the Left M.G. Group, and will be organised into two sub-groups as stated in Appendix "A" attached.
These Batteries will take up their position on the night lst/2nd August and will probably be withdrawn on the night 3rd/4th August.
The above sub-groups will come under the orders of the Left Group Commander, Major E. Naylor, 35th Bn. M.G. Corps forthwith.

4. Nos. 1 and 2 Sections, "D" Company with personnel as stated in Appendix "A" attached, will report to the Right Sub-Group Commander (Major W. R. Lewis) at 12 noon, 31st July at Q.17.d.8.1., and will be accommodated in the forward area under arrangements to be made by him.
Nos. 3 and 4 Sections, "D" Company, with personnel as stated in Appendix "A" attached, will report to the Left Sub-group Commander (Major C. D. Ingram) at 12 noon, 31st July, at R.3.c.0.6., and will be accommodated in the forward area under arrangements to be made by him.
The Roar Headquarters of the 30th Bn. M.G. Corps and of Companies will remain as at present. The location of Battle Headquarters of the 30th Bn. M.G. Corps will probably be with 35th Bn. M.G. Corps.
Details as to the time and date at which Battalion Battle Headquarters will open will be notified in due course.

5. Batteries of the 30th Bn. M.G. Corps will fire a barrage as detailed in Operation Order No. 29. of 35th Bn. M.G. Corps, copies of which have been sent already to each Sub-group Commander.
All further orders concerning this operation will be issued by or through the Commander of the Left M.G. Group.

6. The Medical Officer will make arrangements to establish an R.A.P. with the R.A.P. at M.16.b.4.7., for stretcher-bearers, and for the evacuation of wounded.

7. ACKNOWLEDGE.

W J Lawton [signature]

Captain for
Lieut. Col.

Commanding 30th. Battalion Machine Gun Corps.

Issued by D.R. at 9.45 p.m.

Copy No. 1.) 2.) Battalion Headquarters.
3. 30th Division "G".
4. 30th Division "Q".
5. 35th Division "G".
6. 35th Bn. M.G. Corps.
7. 36th Bn. M.G. Corps.
8. Xth Corps M.G.O.
9. O.C. "A" Company.

Copy No. 10. O.C. "B" Company.
11. " "C" "
12. " "D" "
13. Major. E.E. Naylor (35th Bn. M.G.C.)
14.) 15.) War Diary.
16. File.
17. Spare.

APPENDIX " A "

Issued with 30th. Battalion Machine Gun Corps Order No. 18.

Composition and Locations of Batteries and Headquarters.

Sub. Group.	Battery.	Commander.	No. of Guns.	Composition	Personnel. Sgts.	Cpls.	L/Cpls.	Ptes.	Location of Left. Gun.
Right.	A.	Lt. R. B. Sparrow.	6	4 Guns No. 1 Sec. C Coy. 2 Guns No. 2 Sec. D Coy.	2	3	1	20	M 22 b 8.7
do	B.	Lt. J. J. Pascoe.	6	4 Guns No 2 Sec. C Coy. 2 Guns No. 4 Sec. C Coy.	1	3	2	20	M 22 b 7.9
do	C.	Lt. J. E. Sanderson.	6	4 Guns No. 3 Sec. C Coy. 2 Guns No. 4 Sec. C Coy.	1	3	2	20	M 17 c 05.20
do	D.	Lt. F.C.T. Woodhead.	6	4 Guns No. 1 Sec. D Coy. 2 Guns No. 2 Sec. D Coy.	2	2	2	20	M 17 c 25.35
Sub-Group H. Q. M 16 d 9.5. Commander Major W. R. Lewis. Officers. Lt. T. Trethowan, Lt. J. R. Strong.									
Left.	E	Lt. T. M. Lewis.	6	4 Guns No. 3 Sec. D Coy. 2 Guns No. 4 Sec. D Coy.	2	4	-	20	M 17 c 40.40
do	F	Lt. J. D. Home.	6	4 Guns No. 1 Sec. C Coy. 2 Guns No. 4 Sec. D Coy.	1	5	-	20	M 17 c 85.60
do	G	Lt. N. H. Whiffon.	6	4 Guns No. 2 Sec. C Coy. 2 Guns No. 4 Sec. C Coy.	1	5	-	20	M 17 c 98.85
do	H	Lt. E. M. Dempster.	6	4 Guns No. 3 Sec. C Coy. 2 Guns No. 4 Soc. C Coy.	2	4	-	20	M 17 b 17.00
Sub-Group H. Q. M 16 b 5.5. Commandor Major C. D. Ingram. Officers Capt. J.F.A. Swanston, Lt. W. V. Grigson.									

30th. Battalion Machine Gun Corps Battle Headquarters will probably be with 35th. Battalion Machine Gun Corps
Composition Lieut. Col. H. G. V. Roberts, M. C., Lieut. G. Stevenson, and Bn. H.Q. Scouts.

Note 1. Each Sub-Group Commander will send to 30th. Bn. M. G. Corps Battle Headquarters 3 runners who are thoroughly acquainted with the routes to their respective Sub-Group Headquarters at whatever time theso open.

2. O. C. D Coy. will sond 8 spare men to each Sub-Group, to replace any casualties or sick before Zoro.

SECRET. Copy No. 16

30th Battalion Machine Gun Corps Warning Order No. 19.

Reference Sheets 27. (1/40,000).
BAILLEUL 28. S.W. 3. 1/10,000.
KEMMEL 28. S.W. 1. 1/10,000.

5th. August, 1918.

1. The operation mentioned in 30th Bn. M.G. Corps Order No. 18 will probably take place on the night of the 6/7th August.

2. In the event of orders being received that the operation will be carried out, instructions contained in 30th Bn. M.G. Corps Order No. 18., and 35th Bn. M.G. Corps Order No. 29 will hold good with the following exceptions:-

(a) Batteries of the 30th Bn. M.G. Corps as detailed in Appendix "A" will move into position on the night 5/6th August.
(b) The Left Group Commander will be Major Troup, 35th Bn. M.G. Corps.
(c) The Right Sub-group Commander will be Captain Tresham, 30th Bn. M.G. Corps
(d) Para 6 of 30th Bn. M.G. Corps order No. 18 is cancelled and the following substituted:-

The Medical Officer will make arrangements for Stretcher Bearers and the evacuation of wounded.

(e) Advance Headquarters 30th Bn. M.G. Corps will open at LANCET FARM at 6 p.m., 6th August.

3. In the event of a decision being made that the operation will be carried out, information of this fact will be wired to Company Commanders concerned by the code word "RIGHT".
In the event of the operation being cancelled, the information will be wired to the Company Commanders concerned by the Code word "NAPOO"
Definite information is expected about 5 p.m. to-night, 5th August.
It is hoped that in the event of orders being received to move into position, lorries will be obtained to move the personnel of "D" Company to the Headquarters of "B" & "C" Coy's respectively

4. ACKNOWLEDGE.

W J Fawdes
Captain for
Lieut. Col.

Commanding 30th Battalion Machine Gun Corps.

Issued by D.R. at 11.50 a.m.

Copy No. 1.) Battalion Headquarters.
2.)
3. 30th Division "G".
4. 30th Division "Q".
5. 35th Division "G".
6. 35th Bn. M.G. Corps.
7. 36th Bn. M.G. Corps.
8. Xth Corps M.G.O.
9. O.C. "A" Company.

Copy No. 10. O.C. "B" Company.
11. "C" "
12. "D" "
13. Major Troup. (35th Bn. M.G.C.)
14.) War Diary.
15.)
16. File.
17. Spare.

file

SECRET. Copy No.

30th Battalion Machine Gun Corps Order No. 20.

Reference Sheet. 27 S.E. and 28 S.W. 6th August, 1918.

1. The 30th Division will relieve the 35th Division in the left Sector of Corps Front.

2. The 30th Battalion Machine Gun Corps will be relieved by and will relieve the 35th Battalion Machine Gun Corps in accordance with table attached.

3. Details of relief will be arranged between Company Commanders concerned.

4. Command of the M. Gs. on the Divisional Front will pass to O.C. 30th Battalion Machine Gun Corps on completion of relief on the night 10/11th August.

5. Advanced Headquarters 30th Battalion Machine Gun Corps will open at LANCET FARM R.11.c.9.5. at 7 p.m. 10th inst.

6. ACKNOWLEDGE.

G. Stevens Lieut. & A/Adjutant,
for Lieut. Colonel

Commanding 30th Battalion Machine Gun Corps.

Issued by D.R. at p.m.

Copy No. 1.) Battalion Headquarters.
2.)
3. 30th Division "G".
4. 30th Division "Q".
5. 35th Division "G".
6. 35th Bn. M.G. Corps.
7. 36th Bn. M.G. Corps.
8. Xth Corps M.G.O.
9. 41st Bn. M.G. Corps.
10. A.D.M.S. 30th Division.
11. 30th Divisional Train.
12. O.C. "A" Company.
13. "B" "
14. "C" "
15. "D" "
16.) War Diary.
17.)
18. File.
19. Spare.

30th Battalion Machine Gun Corps.

Appendix to Order No. 20.

	August.	
(1)	7/8.	Reservc Company 35th Battalion M.G.C. will relieve "A" Company 30th Battalion M.G.C. in Second Position. "A" Company will billet for night of 7/8th in quarters of Reserve Company near LANCET FARM. Completion of relief to be notified to Bn. Headquarters by Codo word "MONKEY"
(2)	8/9.	"A" Company 30th Battalion M.G.C. will rolieve Company of 35th Battalion M.G.C. in left Subsector. Completion of relief to be notified to Battalion Headquarters by Code word "PONY".
(3)	10/11	"B" Company 30th Battalion Machine Gun Corps will relieve Company of 35th Battalion M.G.C. in Right Subsoctor. Completion of relief to be notified to Bn. Headquarters by Code words "GOOD LUCK".
(4)	10/11.	"C" Company 30th Battalion M.G.C. will relieve Company of 35th Battalion M.G.C. in Centre Subsector. Completion of rclief to be notified to Battalion Headquarters by Code word "OMNIBUS".
(5)	10/11.	"D" Company 30th Battalion M.G.C. will rolieve Company of 35th Battalion M.G.C. in Reserve near LANCET FARM. Completion of relief to be notified to Battalion Headquarters by Code word "SUNSHINE.

Transport Lines of the 35th Battalion will be taken over by Company Transport on the same night as the Company reliof.

Quartermaster Stores of 35th Battalion will be taken over by Quartermaster of 30th Battalion on 10th inst.

SECRET. Copy No. 2

30th. BATTALION MACHINE GUN CORPS ORDER No. 21.

Reference Sheet, 27. S.E. & 28. S.W. 14th. August, 1918.

1. "D" Company will relieve "A" Company in the Left Group on the night of 15/16th-8-18.

2. Details of the relief will be arranged by the Company Commanders concerned.

3. Completion of relief will be notified to Battalion Advance Headquarters by the code-word "HOPE"

4. On completion of relief "A" Company will be Divisional Reserve, and will be prepared to man Reserve positions as stated in the 30th Battalion Machine Gun Corps' Defence Scheme No. 3 (Provisional)

5. ACKNOWLEDGE.

P.S. Greenwell Lieut A/J
for Lieut. Colonel,
Commanding 30th Battalion Machine Gun Corps.

Issued by D.R. at 10.30 pm.

Copy No. 1.) Battalion Headquarters.
2.)
3. 30th British Division "G".
4. 30th " " "Q".
5. 21st Infantry Brigade.
6. 89th Infantry Brigade.
7. 90th Infantry Brigade.
8. Xth Corps M.G.O.
9. 36th Bn. M.G.C.
10. 41st Bn. M.G.C.
11. C.R.A.
12. C.R.E.
13. A.D.M.S.
14. O.C. "A" Company 30th Bn.
15. O.C. "B" Comapny 30th Bn.
16. O.C. "C" Company 30th Bn.
17. O.C. "D" Company 30th Bn.
18. O.C. Signal Company.
19.) War Diary.
20.)
21. File.
22. Spare.

SECRET. Copy No. 26

30th BATTALION MACHINE GUN CORPS ORDER No. 22.

Reference:- LOCRE MAP 1/10,000. 16th. August, 1918.
Sheet 27 S.E. 1/20,000.
28 S.W. 1/20,000.

1. For the operation detailed in 30th Division Order No. 184, Machine Guns will be divided into "Batteries" and "Pairs". "Pairs" are posts of ~~two~~ two guns not organised into Batteries but able to fire with effect from their present positions.

2. These Batteries and Pairs will be organised into Groups as follows:-

"A" Group. Commander Major A.C. Thorn, 30th Battalion M.G.C. Headquarters with 90th Inf. Brigade at M.22.a.0.1.

"B" Group. Commander Major H. Leah, 35th Battalion M.G.C. Headquarters with 21st Inf. Brigade at M.16.b.4.5.

"C" Group. Commander Major O.M. Parker, 30th Battalion M.G.C. Headquarters with 21st Inf. Brigade at M.16.b.4.5.

Major C.D. Ingram 30th Battalion M.G.C. will be at 89th Infantry Brigade Headquarters and will act as liaison Officer. He will ensure that the wishes of the G.O.C. 89th Infantry Brigade with regard to M.Gs. are carried out.

3. Composition of Groups, Batteries and Pairs, and the tasks allotted to each are shown in Barrage Organization Scheme attached.

4. Group Commanders are responsible for all arrangements for the guns under their Command, for the accuracy of calculation, for the maintenance of the necessary safety clearances and for the synchronisation of the watches of themselves and their subordinate Commanders.

5. The 35th Battalion M.G.C. which is attached for the operation to the 30th Division and "A" Company, 30th Battalion M.G.C. will be in position 24 hours before Zero.

6. The 41st Battalion M.G.C. will co-operate by ~~giving~~ firing concentration on selected points and by firing a Barrage as stated in Barrage Organization Scheme.

7. The 36th Battalion M.G.C. will co-operate by harassing the FOXGLOVE RIDGE S.4.d. and S.5.c. as stated in Barrage Organization Scheme.

8. All Batteries will be ready to fire by Zero - 4 hours. O.C. Groups will report all ready to O.C. 30th Battalion M.G.C. whose Headquarters will be with Advanced Divisional Headquarters at LA MONTAGNE by the code word "BLIGHTY".

9. Particulars re-communications will be issued later.

10. ACKNOWLEDGE.

Lieut. Colonel,

Commanding 30th Battalion Machine Gun Corps.

Issued by D.R. at 6.30.p.m. 16-8-18

Copy No. 1. 30th British Division "G"
2. 30th British Division "A" & "Q".
3. 21st Infantry Brigade.
4. 89th Infantry Brigade.
5. 90th Infantry Brigade.
6. C.R.A. 30th British Div.
7. C.R.E. 30th British Div.
8. O.C. 35th Battalion M.G.C.
9. O.C. 36th Battalion M.G.C.
10. O.C. 41st Battalion M.G.C.
11. Xth Corps M.G.O.
12. O.C. "A" Company, 30th Battalion M.G.C.
13. O.C. "B" Company, 30th Battalion M.G.C.
14. O.C. "C" Company, 30th Battalion M.G.C.
15. O.C. "D" Company, 30th Battalion M.G.C.
16. O.C. "A" Company, 35th Battalion M.G.C.
17. O.C. "B" Company, 35th Battalion M.G.C.
18. O.C. "C" Company, 35th Battalion M.G.C.
19. O.C. "D" Company, 35th Battalion M.G.C.
20. Major O.M. Parker.
21. Major H. Loah.
22. Major A.C. Thorn.
23. Signalling Officer, 30th Battalion M.G.C.
24. O.C. Signals, 30th British Division.
25. A.D.M.S. 30th British Division.
26.) War Diary.
27.)
28. File.
29. Spare.

Barrage Organization Scheme. 30th. Battalion Machine Gun Corps Sheet No. 1.

"A" Group Commander Major A. C. Thorn. Composed of No. 1 & 2 Sub-Groups.

Headquarters M 22 a 0.1

No. 1 Sub-Group Captain C. H. Tresham. Headquarters M 22 a 0.1

Pair or Battery.	Approximate Location of Pair or Battery.	Task.	Time.	S. O. S.	Rate of Fire
"A" (4 guns)	M 22 a 75. 00.	M 35 c 9.2 to M 35 d 3.3	Zero till Zero plus 46.	Same as Task.	Zero to Zero plus 46 100 rounds per minute. S. O. S. 1st. Five minutes 200 rounds per minute, follow-ing 10 minutes 100 rounds per minute, then cease unless again called for.
No. 1 Pair	M 27 c 9.9	S 5 a 2.4 to S 5 a 2.6	Zero till Zero plus 46.	Same as Task.	
No. 2 Pair.	M 27 b 6.3	S 5 a 2.6 to S 5 a 2.8	Zero till Zero plus 46.	Same as Task.	
No. 3 Pair.	M 22 c 15.30	S 5 a 2.8 to M 35 c 2.0	Zero till Zero plus 46.	Same as Task.	
No. 4 Pair.	M 28 a 9.9.	M 35 c 3.2 to M 35 c 5.2	Zero till Zero plus 46.	Same as Task.	
No. 5 Pair.	M 22 d 2.7	M 35 c 5.2 to M 35 c 7.2	Zero till Zero plus 46.	Same as Task.	
No. 6 Pair.	M 22 d 3.8	M 35 c 7.2 to M 35 c 9.2	Zero till Zero plus 46.	Same as Task.	
No. 7 Pair.	M 22 d 85.05	M 35 d 3.3 to M 35 d 5.3	Zero till Zero plus 46.	Same as Task.	
No. 8 Pair.	M 22 b 85.00	N 35 d 5.3 to M 35 d 7.3	Zero till Zero plus 46.	Same as Task.	

Composition No. 1 Sub-Group 4 Gun B Coy. 30th. Battalion Machine Gun Corps

16 Guns C Coy. 30th. Battalion Machine Gun Corps

Barrage Organization Scheme. 30th. Battalion Machine Gun Corps. Sheet No. 2

"A" Group. No. 2 Sub-Group Commander Lieut. L. H. Merricks, 30th. Battalion Machine Gun Corps.

Composition 16 guns "A" Company 30th. Battalion Machine Gun Corps.

Battery.	Approximate Location of Battery.	1st. Task.	Time.	2nd. Task.	Time.	S. O. S.	Rate of Fire.
"B" Battery. 4 Guns.	M 22 c 9.8	M 29 c 3.2 - M 29 c 7.2	Zero till Zero plus 7	M.35.c.3.2 - S.5.a.3.8	Zero plus 8 till Zero plus 46.	Same as Second Task.	Zero till Zero plus 43 100 rounds per minute. S. O. S. First five minutes 200 rounds per minute. Following 10 minutes 100 rounds per minute Then cease unless again called for.
"C" Battery 4 Guns.	M 22 d 1.8	M 35 a 3.8 - M 35 a 7.8	Zero till Zero plus 7.	S.5.a.3.8 - S.5.a.3.4	Zero plus 8 till Zero plus 46.		
"D" Battery 4 Guns.	M 22 d 2.8	M 35 a 3.5 - M 35 a 7.5	Zero till Zero plus 7.	M.35.c.3.2 - M.35.c.7.2	Zero plus 8 till Zero plus 46.		
"E" Battery 4 Guns	M 22 d 80.95	M 35 a 3.2 - M 35 a 7.2	Zero till Zero plus 7.	M.35.c.7.2 - M.35.d.1.2	Zero plus 8 till Zero plus 46.		

Barrage Organization Scheme 30th. Battalion Machine Gun Corps. Sheet No. 3.

"B" Group. Commander Major H. Leah 35th. Battalion Machine Gun Corps. Headquarters M 16 b 4.5.
Composed of No. 3 and No. 4 Sub-Groups.
No. 3 Sub-Group. Commander and Headquarters to be notified later.

Composition 24 Guns of 35th. Battalion Machine Gun Corps.

Battery.	Approximate Location of Battery.	1st. Task.	Time.	2nd. Task.	Time.	3rd. Task.	Time.	S.O.S.	Rate of Fire.
"F" Battery 6 Guns.	M 22 b 7.7	M 29 c 25.40 to M 35 a 25.80	Zero till Zero Plus 6.	M 29 c 9.4 to M 35 a 9.8	Zero plus 6 till Zero plus 15.	M 30 c 0.4 to M 36 a 1.8	Zero plus 15 till Zero plus 46.	Same as Third Task.	100 rounds per minute for 1st. 2nd. and 3rd. Tasks. S. O. S. 200 rounds per minute first Five minutes 100 rounds per minute next ten minutes, then ceases unless again called for.
"G" Battery 6 Guns.	M 22 b 8.9	M 35 a 25.80 to M 35 a 25.20	Zero till Zero Plus 6	M 35 a 9.8 to M 35 a 9.2	Zero plus 6 till Zero plus 15	M 36 a 1.8 to M 36 a 2.2	Zero plus 15 till Zero plus 46.		
"H" Battery. 6 Guns.	M 17 c 2.2	M 29 c 4.4 to M 35 a 4.8	Zero till Zero plus 8	M 29 d 1.4 to M 35 b 1.8	Zero plus 8 till Zero plus 17.	M 30 c 2.5 to M 36 a 5.9	Zero plus 17 till Zero plus 46		
"I" Battery 6 Guns	M 17 c 3.3	M 35 a 4.8 to M 35 a 4.2	Zero till Zero Plus 8	M 35 b 1.8 to M 35 b 1.2	Zero plus 8 till Zero plus 17.	M 36 a 3.9 to M 36 a 4.3	Zero plus 17 till Zero plus 46.		

Barrage Organization Scheme 30th. Battalion Machine Gun Corps. Shoot No. IV. a.

"B" Group.

No. 4 Sub-Group. Commander and Headquarters to be notified lator.

Composition 24 Guns 55th. Battalion Machine Gun Corps.

Battery.	Approximato Location of Battory	1st. Task.	Time.	2nd. Task.	Timo.	3rd. Task.	Time.	S.O.S.	Rate of Firo.
J. Battory. 6 Guns.	M 17 c 4.5	M 29 c 6.4 to M 35 a 6.8	Zero to Zero plus 10.	M 35 b 4.2 to M 35 d 4.6	Zero plus 10 to Zoro plus 20	M 30 c 3.7 to M 30 c 4.1	Zero plus 20 to Zero plus 46.	Samo as 3rd. Task.	100 rounds per minute for 1st., 2nd. & 3rd. Task. S.O.S. 200 rounds per minute 1st. 5 minutes. 100 rounds per minute succeding 10. minutes. Then ceases unless again called for.
K. Battery. 6 Guns.	M 17 c 8.6	M 35 a 6.8 to M 35 a 6.2	Zero to Zero plus 10.	M 35 b 4.8 to M 35 b 4.2	Zero plus 10 to Zoro plus 20	M 30 c 4.1 to M 36 a 5.5	Zero plus 20 to Zorc plus 46.		
L. Battery 6 Guns.	M 17 d 0.9	M 29 c 8.4 to M 35 a 8.8	Zoro to Zero plus 12.	M 35 b 5.2 to M 35 d 5.6	Zero plus 10 to Zoro plus 20.	M 30 c 5.8 to M 30 c 7.2	Zero plus 20 to Zero plus 46.		
M. Battery 6 Guns.	M 17 b 2.1	M 35 a 8.8 to M 35 a 8.2	Zero to Zero plus 12.	M 35 b 5.8 to M 35 b 5.2	Zoro plus 10 to Zero plus 20.	M 30 c 7.2 to M 36 a 8.6	Zero plus 20 to Zero plus 46.		

Barrage Organization Schemo 30th. Battalion Machine Gun Corps. Sheet No. V.a.

"C" Group. Commander Major O. M. Parkor, 30th. Battalion Machine Gun Corps.

Headquarters M 16 b 4.5 Composed of No. 5 & 6 Sub-Groups.

No. 5.. Subgroup Hoadquartors and Commander to be notified later.

Composition "D" Company 35th. Battalion Machino Gun Corps. (16 Guns.)

Battory.	Approximate Location of Battery.	1st. Task.	Time.	2nd. Task.	Timo.	S. O. S.	Rate of Firo.
N. Battery 4 Guns.	M 23 a 4.6	M 35 d 4.8 to M 35 d 8.8	Zero to Zero plus 20.	M 35 d 1.3 to M 35 d 5.5	Zero plus 20 to Zoro plus 46	Same as Second Task.	1st. & 2nd. Task 100 rounds per minute. S. O. S. First Five minutos 200 rounds per minutc. Suceeding 10 minutes 100 rounds per minute. Thon cease fire unloss again called for.
O. Battery 4 Guns.	M 23 a 5.6	M 35 b 6.8 to M 36 a 0.8	Zero to Zero plus 20.	M 35 d 5.5 to M 35 d 8.8	Zero plus 20 to Zoro plus 46		
P. Battory. 4 Guns.	M 23 a 6.7	M 35 d 8.8 to M 36 a 1.1	Zero to Zero plus 46				
Q. Battery 4. Guns.	M 23 a 7.8	M 36 a 1.1 to M 36 a 4.3	Zero to Zero plus 46				

Barrage Organization Scheme 30th. Battalion Machine Gun Corps. Sheet No. VI. a.

"C" Group.

No. 6 Sub-Group. Commander Captain P.G. Walsh, 30th. Battalion Machine Gun Corps.

Headquarters M 22 b 6.6

Composition "D" Company 30th. Battalion Machine Gun Corps. (16 Guns.)

Battery.	Approximate Location of Battery.	1st. Task.	Time.	2nd. Task.	Time.	S.O.S.	Rate of Fire
R. Battery. 6 Guns.	M 22 b 6.6	Harass area formed by joining following points M 35 b 6.8 M 35 b 6.2 M 36 a 0.2 M 36 a 0.8	Zero to Zero plus 20.	M 35 b 95.10 to M 36 a 35.80	Zero plus 20 to Zero plus 46.	Same as 2nd. Task.	Zero to Zero plus 10 100 rounds per minute. Zero plus 10 to Zero plus 35 75 rounds per minute. Zero plus 35 to Zero plus 46 100 rounds per minute. S.O.S. First Five minutes 200 rounds per minute. Suceeding 10 minutes 100 rounds per minute. Then cease unless again called for.
S. Battery 4 Guns.	M 17 d 1.2	Harass Area formed by joining following points. M 35 b 6.2 M 35 d 6.8 M 36 c 0.8 M 36 a 0.2	Zero to Zero plus 20.	M 36 a 35.80 to M 30 c 75.10	Zero plus 20 to Zero plus 46.		
T. Battery 4 Guns.	M 18 c 5.7	Harass Area formed by joining following points. M 36 a 0.8 M 36 a 0.2 M.36.a.4.2. M 36 a 4.8	Zero to Zero plus 30.	M 30 c 55.55 to M 30 c 85.90	Zero plus 30 to Zero plus 46.		

2 Guns of this Sub-Group will be located as direct Fire guns at about M 24 c 3.5 to cover valley in M 30 a & c. These guns will be silent unless a visable target is seen. All the Batteries of this Sub-Group are Batteries of opportunity ready to switch on to any target within range on receipt of orders and able to observe the ground in M 29 d , M 35 b , M 30 a & c , M 36 a.

Barrage Organization Scheme   30th. Battalion Machine Gun Corps.   Sheet No. V11.

Guns of the 56th. Battalion Machine Gun Corps will co-operate by harassing the

FOXGLOVE RIDGE as follows;-

Zero to Zero plus 46 Bursts of Fire of 50 rounds per gun every two minutes.

Dawn till 5-45 a.m. Heavy Harassing Fire.

5-45 a.m. till dusk Occasional bursts of Harassing fire.

Should enemy Artillery Fire become heavy on DRANOUTRE RIDGE or S. O. S. be sent up, heavy harassing fire will be opened.

----

8 guns of 41st. Battalion Machine Gun Corps will co-operate by firing on selected targets in squares M 30 a & c and M 36 a from Zero till Zero plus 30.

At Zero plus 30 they will barrage on the line M 30 a 7.2 to M 30 d 1.1 *until zero plus 46*

If S. O. S. is sent up they will barrage on this same line.

Copy No. 30.

SECRET.

Addenda & Corrigenda to 30th. Battalion Machine Gun Corps Operation Order No. 22.

(a) Countor Preparation.

All Batteries and Pairs will fire 250 rounds per gun rapid on their S. O. S. lines on the night following the attack at the following hours 9-45 p.m., 10-47 p.m., 11-30 p.m., 12-15 a.m. 1-35 a.m., 2-23 a.m., 3-12 a.m.

At 3-45 a.m. on the morning following the attack all Batteries and Pairs will fire for 3 minutes on their S. O. S. lino Ratc of Fire First minute 250 rounds per minute Following two minutes 125 rounds per minute.

(b) Sheets lV. V. and Vl. of Barrage Organization Scheme are cancelled and will be destroyed forthwith and sheets lV.a, V.a, and Vl.a, attached will bc substituted.

(c) Roference Sheet No. 1. Barrage Organization Scheme, Delete Tasks for No. 1., No. 2, and No. 3 Pairs and substituto:-

No. 1. Pair	Task	S.5 a 5.4	to	S. 5 a 5.6
No. 2. Pair	Task	S. 5 a 5.6	to	S. 5 a 5.8
No. 3. Pair	Task	S. 5 a 5.8	to	M. 35 c 50.00.

(d) Acknowledge.

P.S. Greenwell
Lt Adj for Lieut. Col.
Commanding 30th. Battalion Machine Gun Corps.

Issued by D. R. at 2 pm. 18-8-18

Copies to all recipients of Order No. 22.

Code Names in use during 30th Battn. M.G.C. Barrage Scheme.

....

O.C. 30th Battn. M.G.Corps. . . . . GAGO C/o JERA

Major Ingram (Liaision Officer) . . . . 2 GAGO C/o BUVO

Major Thorn (O.C."A"Group) . . . . 1 GAGO C/o BUJO

O.C. No. 1. Sub-Group - Communication direct from Group Commdr.

O.C. No. 2. Sub-Group - Communication through ZARI

Major Leah. (O.C."B" Group) . . . . KOWI C/o BUPI

O.C. No 3 Sub-Group, Communication direct from Group Commander.

O.C. No 4 SUB-Group, " " " " "

Major Parker. (O.C."C" Group) . . . . 4 GAGO C/o BUPI

~~O.C. No 5 Sub-Group, Communication direct from Group Commander~~

O.C. No 5 Sub-Group, Communication by runner from Group Commander.

O.C. No 6 Sub-Group, Communication direct from Group Commander.

Group Commanders will not need Code names for Sub-group Commanders, having in each case direct communication, except in one case, viz-- O.C. "A" group has communication to O.C. No 2 Sub-group through ZARI,. The address in this case will be GAGO C/o ZARI.

20th August 1918.

E A Webster
signal officer

Secret.

To.- O.C. 36th Bn. M.G.Corps.
O.C. 41st Bn. M.G.Corps.
Lieut. Webster.
Major Leah.
Major O.M.Parker.
Major Thorn.
O.C."A" Coy.-)
"B" Coy.)
"C" Coy.)30th Bn.
"D" Coy.)M.G.Corps
O.C."A" Coy.)
"B" Coy.)
"C" Coy.)35th Bn.
"D" Coy.)M.G.Corps.

With reference to 30th Battalion Machine Gun Corps operation order No. 22., the following instructions re S.O.S. and Synchronization of Watches are issued.

1. S.O.S.

A Special S.O.S. Rifle Grenade, GREEN/GREEN/GREEN will be used in the case of hostile attack on the captured ground, to call for the protection barrage.

This Signal will be in force from ZERO + 50 minutes, until 6.am. on the 2nd day after ZERO, after which the ordinary Signal will come into force on the battle front.

The ordinary Signal, RED/RED/RED will be used in case of an attack on any partion of the Divisional Front from which the advance has not been made.

2. SYNCHRONIZATION OF WATCHES.

Group Commanders, "A" "B" and "C" Groups, will attend 90th Infantry Brigade Headquarters at M.22.a.o.1 on ZERO - 1 day, at 3.pm, and will synchronize their watches with a Divisional Staff Officer who will be there for that purpose.

Group Commanders are responsible for the Synchronization of the watches of their Sub-Group Commanders and Battery Commanders.

Lieut. Webster will attend at the same place and hour to Synchronize for 30th Bn. M.G.C. Headquarters.

3. Acknowledge.

Lieut. Col.

18th August 1918. Commanding 30th Battalion Machine Gun Corps.

Signal Communications for Barrage Scheme
30 Battalion M.G.C.

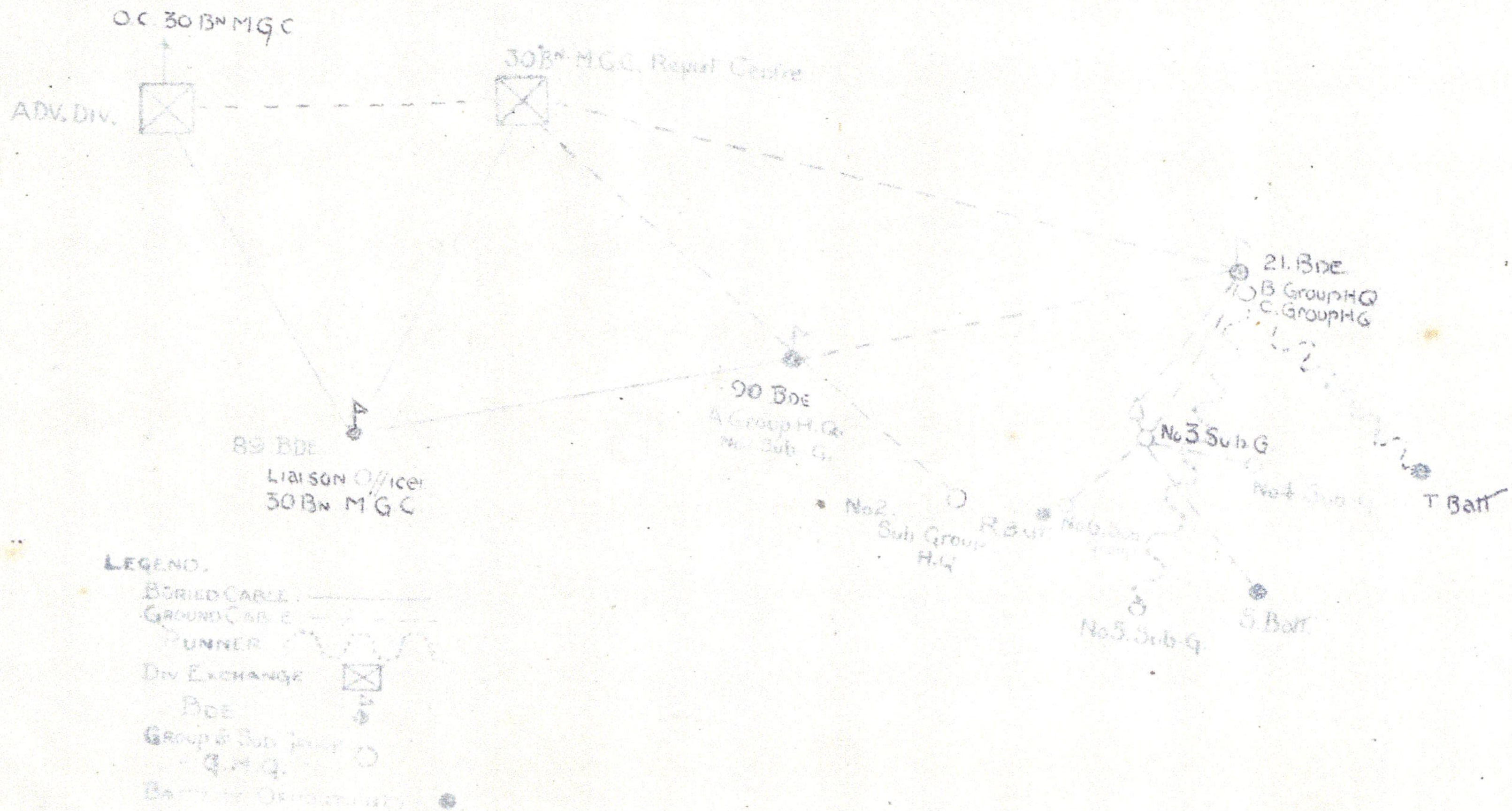

30th Battalion Machine Gun Corps. No.22/22/A

To,

All recepients of 30th Battalion M.G.Corps order No. 22.

The following Amendments to Barrage Organisation Scheme attached to the above order are made.

SHEET No. 1.

No. 1 Pair.	Delete Task stated and substitute	-	S.5.a.5.4	to S.5.a.5.6
No. 2 Pair.	" " " " "		S.5.a.5.6	to S.5.a.5.8
No. 3 Pair.	" " " " "		S.5.a.5.8	to M.35.c.5.0
No. 4 Pair.	" " " " "		M.35.c.5.2	to M.35.c.7.2

SHEET No. 2.

"B" Battery.	Delete 2nd Task and substitute	- -	M.35.c.5.2	to S.5.a.5.8
"C" Battery.	" " " " "	- -	S.5.a.5.8	to S.5.a.5.4
"D" Battery.	" " " " "	- -	M.35.c.7.2	to M.35.d.1.2
"E" Battery.	" " " " "	- -	M.35.d.1.2	to M.35.d.5.2

SHEET IVa.

"J" Battery.	Delete 2nd Task and substitute	-	M.35.b.4.4	to M.35.d.4.9
"L" Battery.	" " " " "	-	M.35.b.5.8	to M.35.b.5.2

Times for Tasks unaltered.

....

P.L. Greenwell Lt A/Adj for Lieut. Col.

19th August 1918. Commanding 30th Battalion Machine Gun Corps.

SECRET. *File* Copy. *26*.......

30th Battalion Machine Gun Corps Order No. 23.

....

Reference Map. LOCRE 1/10,000. 21st August 1918.

1. All Companies of the 35th Battalion Machine Gun Corps will come under the command of Major LEAH forthwith.
These will be withdrawn under orders to be issued by him, to their transport lines as soon as possible after dusk on the evening of the *22nd* inst.
Major LEAH will report as early as possible to LANCET FARM where further instructions as to the move of the 35th Battalion Machine Gun Corps to the back area will be issued to him.

2. As soon as possible after dusk on the *22nd* inst, "A" Company 30th Battalion Machine Gun Corps will be withdrawn to its previous billets near LANCET FARM and will resume the duties of M.G.Company in Divisional Reserve.

3. "B" "C" and "D" Companies will again form the RIGHT, CENTRE and LEFT Groups respectively. Their S.O.S. will be adjusted forthwith as stated in the table attached to this order.
Group Commanders are responsible that the necessary clearances over our front line are maintained.

4. O.C. RIGHT Group will reconnoitre forthwith positions on the two spurs running from M.21 to M.27 with a view to pushing up four out of the eight guns at present located in M.20 and M.21 to more forward positions covering the BLUE LINES and capable of participating in the S.O.S. Barrage.

5. Acknowledge,.

R.J. Greenwell Lieut & A/Adj
for Lieut. Col.
Commanding 30th Battalion Machine Gun Corps.

Issued by D.R. at *1-0 a.m. 22-8-18*

Copy No 1. 30th Division "G"
2. 30th Division "A" & "Q"
3. 21st Infantry Brigade
4. 89th Infantry Brigade
5. 90th Infantry Brigade
6. C.R.A. 30th Division
7. C.R.E. 30th Division
8. O.C. 35th Bn. M.G.C.
9. O.C. 36th Bn. M.G.C.
10. O.C. 41st Bn. M.G.C.
11. Xth Corps M.G.O.
12. O.C. "A" Coy.) 30th Bn. M.G.C.
13. O.C. "B" Coy.)
14. O.C. "C" Coy.)
15. O.C. "D" Coy.)

Copy No 16. O.C. "A" Coy.) 35th Battalion M.G.Corps.
17. O.C. "B" Coy.)
18. O.C. "C" Coy.)
19. O.C. "D" Coy.)
20. Major Parker.
21. Major Leah
22. Major Thorn.
23. O.C. Signals 30th Division
24.) War Diary
25.)
26. File
27. Spare

30th Battalion M. G. Corps, Order No 23 - Appendix 1.

S.O.S. Scheme to be taken into force forthwith.

The following Guns only will have S.O.S. Lines.

RIGHT Group.

2 Guns at M.27.c.9.9	(approx)	S.O.S.Line	M.35.d.45.35	- M.35.d.60.45
2 Guns at (M.27.b.9.3) (M.27.b.5.3)	"	"	M.35.d.25.20	- M.35.d.45.35
2 Guns at M.28.c.40.95	"	"	S.5.a.80.70	- S.5.a.95.90

CENTRE Group.

2 Guns at M.22.c.20.30	(approx)	S.O.S.Line	M.35.d.60.45	- M.35.d.75.60
4 Guns at M.22.c.28.68	"	"	S.5.a.95.90	- M.35.d.25.20
2 Guns at M.28.a.85.95	"	"	M.35.d.75.60	- M.35.d.90.70
2 Guns at M.22.d.07.68	"	"	M.36.a.2.3	- M.36.a.3.5
2 Guns at M.22.d.9.2	"	"	M.36.a.10.15	- M.36.a.2.3
2 Guns at M.23.c.05.55	"	"	M.35.d.90.70	- M.36.c.05.95
2 Guns at M.22.b.9.5	"	"	M.36.c.05.95	- M.36.a.10.15

LEFT Group.

6 Guns at M.22.b.90.75	(approx)	S.O.S.Line	M.30.c.40.60	- M.30.a.80.00
4 Guns at M.17.d.15.25	"	"	M.30.c.40.60	- M.30.c.40.00
4 Guns at M.17.d.20.25	"	"	M.30.c.40.00	- M.36.a.3.5

Copies only to 30th Division "G" O.C. "A" Coy.)
21st Infantry Brigade "B" Coy.)
89th Infantry Brigade "C" Coy.)30th Battalion
90th Infantry Brigade "D" Coy.) M. G. Corps.
C.R.A. 30th Division O.C. 36th Battn M. G. Corps.
Xth Corps M.G.O. O.C. 41st Battn M. G. Corps.

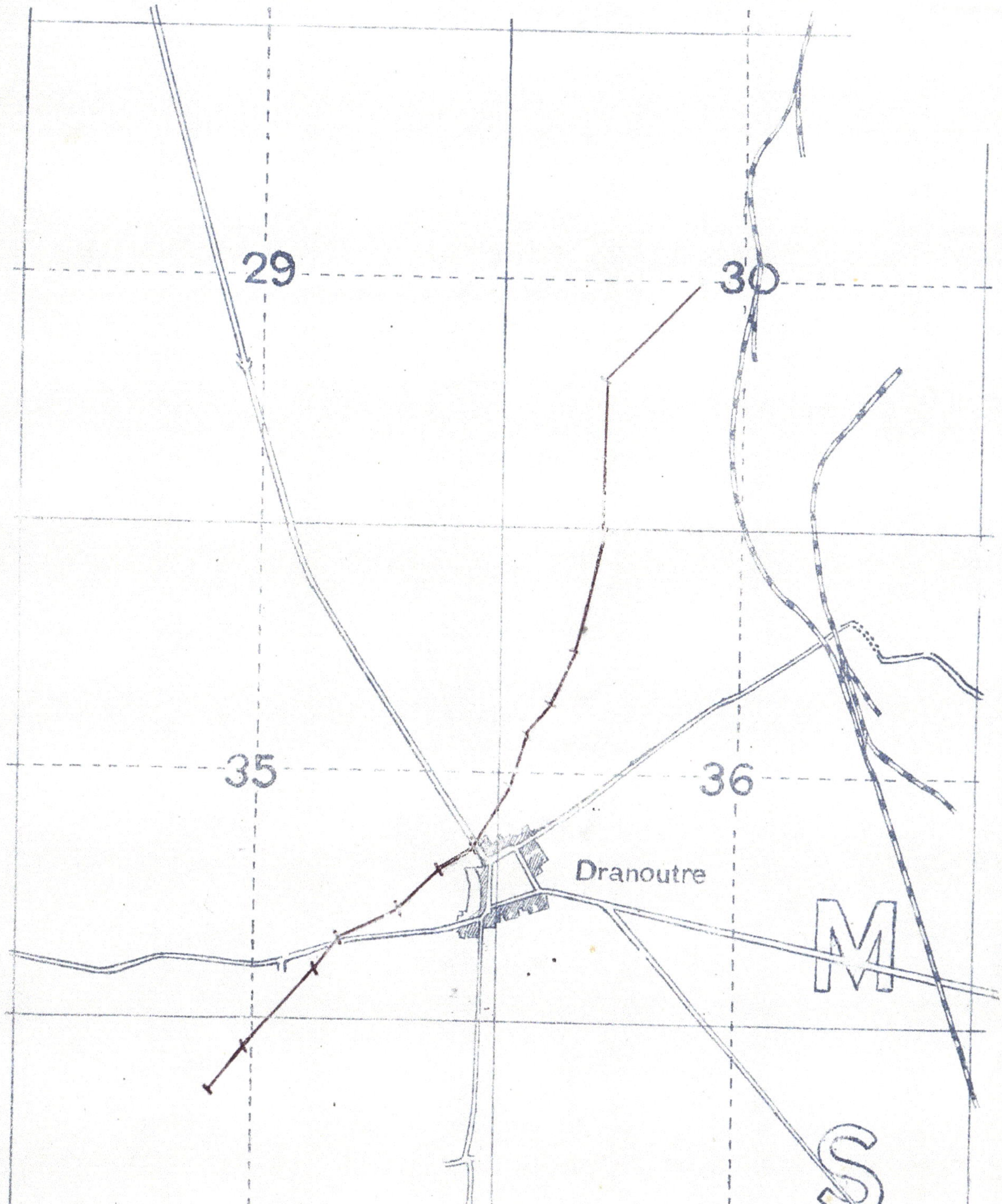

29
30
35
36
Dranoutre
M
S
5
6

SECRET. Copy No. 9

30th BATTALION MACHINE GUN CORPS ORDER No. 24.

25th August, 1918.

1. "A" Company, 30th Battalion Machine Gun Corps will relieve "C" Company, 30th Battalion Machine Gun Corps in the centre sector of the Divisional front during the night 27/28th. August, 1918.

2. All details of the relief will be arranged direct between O's. C. Companies concerned.
O.C. "A" Company will arrange for a thorough reconnaissance of the positions to be taken over previous to the night of the relief.

3. All maps, trench stores, shelters &c., will be handed over and receipts rendered to this Office.
O.C. "C" Company will inform O.C. "A" Company of work in progress and harassing fire programme to be carried out.

4. Completion of relief will be notified by the code word "OKAY".

5. ACKNOWLEDGE.

W J Hawkes
Captain for
Major,
Commanding 30th Battalion Machine Gun Corps.

Issued by D.R. at 8 a. m. 26-8-18

Copy No. 1. O.C. "A" Company.
2. "B" "
3. "C" "
4. "D" "
5. Quartermaster.
6. Signalling Officer.
7. War Diary.
8. " "
9. File.
10. Spare.

Original

Confidential

Vol 7

War Diary

of

30th Battalion Machine Gun Corps

For the month of September 1918

Volume 5

1-30 Sept 1918

Army Form C. 2118.

Instructions regarding War Diaries and Intelligence Summaries are contained in F. S. Regs., Part II. and the Staff Manual respectively. Title pages will be prepared in manuscript.

WAR DIARY
or
INTELLIGENCE SUMMARY.

(Erase heading not required.)

Place	Date	Hour	Summary of Events and Information	Remarks and references to Appendices
LANCET FARM.	1/9/18.		An attack made on NEUVE EGLISE failed owing to the enemy's strong machine gun defence. Battalion Headquarters opened at LANCET FARM at 1 p.m. The Adjutant proceeded to Forward Headquarters on MT VIDAIGNE. Battalion Quartermaster's Stores moved up to WESTOUTRE.	
	2/9/18.		At 1-30 a.m. a second attack was made on NEUVE EGLISE and two Companies of the Inniskilling Fusiliers supported by 2 Sections of "B" Company under Lieuts. Home and Grigson passed through the village and established themselves about 1,000 yards to the East of it. Six Guns of "C" Company were sent from the Divisional Right Front and sited on the ridge East of WULVERGHEM.	
	3/9/18.		In accordance with operation order No. 25 "A" Company relieved "C" Company. Lieut. March's Battery sited near FRENCHMAN'S FARM and Lieut. Elford's North East of WULVERGHEM.	O.O.25
	4/9/18.		Ammunition dumps made as far forward as possible. Numerous Anti-Tank mines discovered and caused many casualties. The mines were laid in iron rectangular boxes about 18" X 10" X 4" in dimensions.	
	5/9/18.		Enemy shelled WULVERGHEM - DAYLIGHT CORNER Road, otherwise fairly quiet.	
	6/9/18.		In accordance with order No. 26. "A" Company took up positions for the defence of the front line and "C" Company and "B" Company, less 2 Sections returned to MT VIDAIGNE.	O.O.26
	7/9/18.		"A" Company put down a short barrage to cover a minor operation. O's. C. "C" & "D" Companies reconnoitred Divisional Front including extension Southwards mentioned in order No. 27. Battalion Rear Headquarters moved up to VIDAIGNE.	O.O.27
MT. VIDAIGNE	8/9/18.		"C" Company moved into the line at dusk in accordance with Order No. 28. and the section of "B" Company quartered in the vicinity of DAYLIGHT CORNER withdrew to MT. VIDAIGNE.	O.O.28
	9/9/18.		"D" Company relieved "A" in the front line in accordance with Battalion Order No. 29. The Commanding Officer returned from leave.	O.O.29
	10/9/18.		A gap in our line was closed during night 9th/10th. Captain J.F.A. Swanston appointed to the Commandof "C" Company. The following reinforcing Officers reported for duty and were posted as follows:- Captain C.S. Nelson, M.C. to be Second in Command of "B" Company. Lieut. W.R. Newenham to "C" Company, 2nd Lieut. H.S.A. Moore to "B" Company, 2nd Lieut. S.W. Kelty to "D" Company. Lieut. Blackwell of the Xth Corps Infantry School and a Sergeant Instructor from the same school attached to the Battalion for 3 days in order to gain an insight into the Machine Gunners "View of things".	
	11/9/18.		Very little activity on either side.	
	12/9/18.		Except for sniping and occasional artillery activity, both sides quiet.	
	13/9/18.		"C" & "D" Company Headquarters shelled during the night, otherwise both sides quiet. "A" & "B" at MT. VIDAIGNE carried on with Company training. Lieut. Blackwell returned to Xth Corps School.	

D. D. & L., London, E.C.
(10340) Wt W5300/P713 750,000 3/18 E 2688 Forms/C2118/16.

Instructions regarding War Diaries and Intelligence Summaries are contained in F. S. Regs., Part II. and the Staff Manual respectively. Title pages will be prepared in manuscript.

WAR DIARY
or
INTELLIGENCE SUMMARY.
(Erase heading not required.)

Army Form C. 2118.

Place	Date	Hour	Summary of Events and Information	Remarks and references to Appendices
MT. VIDAIGNE.	14/9/18.		Situation unchanged. Rev.H.G. ~~Major~~ Crabtree, C.F. came to live with Headquarters.	
	15/9/18.		Church Service at MT. VIDAIGNE.	
	16/9/18.		Inter-Company relief commenced after dusk, "B" Company relieving "D" Company in Rear Sub-group, and "D" Company relieving "C" Company in Forward Sub-group.	
	17/9/18.		Situation quiet and unchanged.	
	18/9/18.		Everything quiet, orders for Division to take over the front of the whole Corps received.	
	19/9/18.		A draft of 67 O.R's arrived from the Base. Two Sections of "D" Company relieved three of "B" in accordance with order No. 33.	
	20/9/18.		Eight guns of "D" Company took part in a minor operation, which took place during night of 20/21st. ~~which~~ Stuck was completely successful. The 1/6th Cheshire Regiment carried their objective under cover of a smoke and Machine Gun Barrage, 14 prisoners were taken including 1 Sergeant Major, 1 Sergeant. Infantry Casualties 3 O.R's killed, 3 O.R's wounded, the Battalion had none.	
	21/9/18.		No change in the situation. "A" Company carried out a practice scheme and "C" Company moved from MT. VIDAIGNE to ST. JANS CAPPEL. During night 20/21st "B" Company took over the positions of the 36th Bn. M.G. Corps.	
	22/9/18.		Situation unchanged.	
	23/9/18.		Situation unchanged.	
	24/9/18.		Except for a minor Raid situation unchanged.	
	25/9/18.		Two minor raids carried out on the Divisional Front, "B" Company supported the one on the right.	
	26/9/18.		Situation unchanged.	
MT. KEMMEL	27/9/18.		Battalion Headquarters (Rear) moved to KEMMEL HILL, Advanced Headquarters moved to ARMOUR FARM near DAYLIGHT FARM.	
	28/9/18.		"B" "C" & "D" Companies assisted the attacks of strong patrols on enemy strong Posts in front of MESSINES RIDGE. They also took advantage of several visible targets on the Ridge. "A" Company moved forward ready to consolidate MESSINES RIDGE as soon as it should be occupied.	Order No. 35 " " 36
	29/9/18.		"A" Company moved forward and consolidated the forward slopes of MESSINES RIDGE soon after it was made good by the Infantry. "B" Company pushed eight guns forward to cover the DOUVE VALLEY. Advanced Headquarters moved to MOULIN DE L'HOSPICE on the MESSINES RIDGE.	Order No.37.

D. D. & L., London, E.C.
(10340) Wt W5300/P713 750,000 3/18 E 2688 Forms/C2118/16.

Army Form C. 2118.

WAR DIARY
or
INTELLIGENCE SUMMARY.
(*Erase heading not required.*)

Instructions regarding War Diaries and Intelligence Summaries are contained in F. S. Regs., Part II. and the Staff Manual respectively. Title pages will be prepared in manuscript.

Place	Date	Hour	Summary of Events and Information	Remarks and references to Appendices
MT. KEMMEL.	30/9/18.		Divisional front changed from facing East to facing South. "C" Company was moved up and became Forward Company, while "A" swung round and took up positions about 1,000x in rear of "C" Company. "B" Company withdrew from the line and concentrated in MESSINES and about 4 p.m. were ordered to move to HOUTHEM, as the Division were taking over the 41st Divisional Front at 10 a.m. "D" Company was in Reserve at S. MIDLAND FARM. Advanced Headquarters moved to dugouts about 300x East of MESSINES on MESSINES - COMINES ROAD.	
			[illegible] Lieut. Colonel,	
			5th October, 1918. Commanding 30th Battalion Machine Gun Corps.	

D. D. & L., London, E.C.
(10340) Wt W5300/P713 750,000 3/18 E 2688 Forms/C2118/16.

Original   Confidential

Appendix

of

War Diary

for

30th Battalion Machine Gun Corps

For the Month of September 1918

Volume 5   1-30 September, 1918

SECRET. Copy No:..7....

Operation Order No. 25.

by

Major O. M. Parker, Temporally Commanding 30th Battalion Machine Gun Corps.

3rd Sept. 1918.

1. "C" Company will relieve "A" Company in the "Line of Resistance" from DONEGAL FARM (N.31.d.) to T. 7.b.9.4. in accordance with verbal instructions to Company Commanders issued this morning.

2. The object of this line is to give a definite "Line of Resistance" and Rallying Point in case of Hostile attack.
"C" Company will remain in this position until further orders from O.C.30th Battn. M.G.Corps.

3. "A" Company will move into positions from which adequate support can be given to the advancing Infantry and will act as " "Batteries of Opportunity".

4. O.C. "A" Company will make his Headquarters at or near the Headquarters of the leading Brigade and will keep in close liason with the B.G.C. He will be in direct telephonic communication with his Batteries.

5. Zero lines will be made out and fighting maps prepared so that targets can be engaged without loss of time.

6. O.C. "A" Company will use his own discretion as to advancing his Batteries so as to keep in close support of Infantry.

7. Special care will be taken to get exact information as to the positions of our own troops.

8. O. C. "A" Company will report when in position giving approximate locality of his Batteries. All subsequent moves will be reported to these Headquarters.

O. M. Parker

Major.

Temporally. Commanding 30th Battalion Machine Gun Corps.

Copy No. 1. 30th Division.
2. 90th Infantry Brigade.
3. O.C. "A" Company.
4. O.C. "C" Company.
5. Quartermaster (for information to Transport Officers.)
6. File.
7. } WAR DIARY
8. }

Copies 3, 4, and 5 to be acknowledged.

P.S. Refce. Para. 4 O.C. "A" Company will be in telephonic communication with leading Brigade if unable to make his Headquarters at or near that place.

SECRET. Copy No....7......

30th Battalion Machine Gun Corps Order No. 26.

....

5th September, 1918.

1. "A" Company will take up positions for the defence of the front line.

Location of battery positions and Company Headquarters will be notified to this Office as early as possible.

ZERO and S.O.S. Lines will be laid out as usual.

2. "C" Company will return to M.21.a.2.0. as soon as necessary transport arrives.

Transport Officer of "C" Company will arrange for the necessary vehicles for relief to be sent at once.

3. The 2 Sections of "B" Company attached to the 89th Brigade will return to M.21.a.2.2. at once.

O.C. "B" Company will make the necessary arrangements for transport.

O.C. "B" Company will move his Headquarters to M.21.a.2.2. at 8 a.m. to-morrow.

4. The working party of the 90th Brigade will remain at its present location and will be at the disposal of O.C. "A" Company.

O.C. "A" Company will be responsible for the rationing of this party.

5. O.C. Companies will report completion of moves to this Office.

6. ACKNOWLEDGE.

T. M. Parker

Major,

Temporally. Commanding 30th Battalion Machine Gun Corps.

Issued by Runner at 11.10 p.m.

Copy No. 1. O.C. "A" Company
2. O.C. "B" "
3. O.C. "C" "
4. Quartermaster.
5. Transport Officer "C" Company.
6. 89th Infantry Brigade.
8. } WAR DIARY

SECRET. Copy No.......8.....

30th Battalion Machine Gun Corps Order No. 27.

7th Sept. 1918.

The following is extracted from 30th Division Order No. 190. -

1. " The following moves of the Infantry will take place:-

(a) On night 8th/9th September, 89th Infantry Brigade will relieve 90th Infantry Brigade in the forward area, the latter after relief proceeding to Support Area about M.28, 29, 34 and 35.

(b) On 9th and 10th September, 21st Infantry Brigade will move from reserve to Support Area and 90th Infantry Brigade from Support to Reserve.

2. (a) The Divisional Area will be at an early date extended Southwards as far as the Railway Line running through U.7. Cent. and T.12. Central.

90th Infantry Brigade will be ready to take this over at short notice and 89th Infantry Brigade must include it in their reconnaissance in case the extention takes place after the relief mentioned in para 1 (a) above.

(b) The MAIN LINE of resistance for the Division will be the line of trenches running East of the NEUVE EGLISE - KEMMEL Road from Divisional Southern Boundary through DE KENNEBAK to neighbourhood of DAYLIGHT CAMP.

3. When the Divisional Area is extended, the 2 Sections of M.Gs. allotted to the forward Brigade will revert to their Battalion and the O.C. 30th Battalion M.G.Corps will arrange the M.G. Defense with 2 Coys., the remaining 2 Coys being in the Reserve Area."

4. "D" Company will be prepared to relieve "A" Company on the night of the 8th/9th or the 9th/10th September.

5. "C" Company will be prepared to move into the line at short notice, when the Divisional Southern Boundary is changed as notified in para 2 (a) above.

6. O's.C. "C" and "D" Companies will immediately make reconnaissances of the Divisional Front to include the extension Southwards. These reconnaissances will be made in conjunction, and O.C. "A" Company will be conferred with by both the above Company Commanders, so that the new dispositions may be made without confusion either before or after the relief of "A" Company by "D" Company.

7. Acknowledge.

W. J. Lawler Capt
for Major.
Temporarily Commanding 30th Battlion Machine Gun Corps.

Issued by runner at 7 a.m.

Copy No. 1 O.C. "A" Coy.
2 O.C. "B" Coy.
3 O.C. "C" Coy.
4. O.C. "D" Coy.
5 Commanding Officer.

Copy No. 6 Quartermaster.
7 File.
8) War Diary.
9)

SECRET. Copy No. 9

30th Battalion Machine Gun Corps Order No. 28.

8th September, 1918.

1. In accordance with 30th Division Order No. 190, "C" Company, 30th Battalion M.G. Corps will relieve on the night 8/9th September, guns of the 36th Battalion M.G. Corps as follows:-

T.7.a.5.8. (2 guns)
T.12.c.9.8. (2 guns)
T.12.b.2.1. (2 guns)
* U.1.a.2.1. (2 guns)

* These guns will be emplaced in new position at T.6.d.7.8.

2. The remaining 8 guns of "C" Company will be emplaced in two batteries:-

4 guns in vicinity of N.34.c.1.7.
4 guns in vicinity of T.4.a.2.2.

3. These locations are temporary only, and are liable to alteration when the M.G. Defence Scheme for the Divisional front is completed.

4. "C" Company Headquarters will, for the present, be at KANDAHAR FARM T.10.a.8.4. As soon as possible O.C. "C" Company will establish his Headquarters at or near those of the Infantry Brigade holding his Sector of the front, and will get into telephonic Communication with them and with 30th M.G. Battalion Headquarters,

5. The Section of "B" Company 30th Bn. M.G. Corps disposed in the vicinity of DAYLIGHT CORNER will withdraw on the night 8/9th September, to their Company bivouacs at MONT VIDAIGNE.

6. Completion of relief and withdrawal will be notified to this Office by runner.

7. ACKNOWLEDGE.

W Hawkes.

Captain for Major,

Temporally. Commanding 30th Battalion Machine Gun Corps.

Issued by D.R. at 8.25 p.m.

Copy No. 1. 30th British Division "G".
2. 36th Battalion M.G.C.
3. O.C. "A" Company 30th. Bn.
4. " "B" " " "
5. " "C" " " "
6. " "D" " " "
7. Quartermaster, 30th Bn.
8. Signalling Officer.
9. War Diary.
10. " "
11. File.
12. Spare.
13 89th Infantry Brigade

SECRET. Copy No.

30th Battalion Machine Gun Corps Order No. 29.

Reference Sheet. 28 N.W. 1/20,000. 9th September, 1918.

1. "D" Company, 30th Battalion Machine Gun Corps will relieve "A" Company, 30th Battalion Machine Gun Corps in the Left Sector of the Divisional Front to-night.

2. Guides of "A" Company will meet the relieving Company at DAYLIGHT CORNER at 10 p.m.

3. Section Officers of "A" Company will give full information to those of "D" Company concerning their front, fields of fire, dispositions of the Infantry &c.

4. "A" Company on relief, will march to billets vacated by "D" Company in WESTOUTRE, and will be in Divisional Reserve.

5. Completion of relief will be notified to this Office by runner.

6. ACKNOWLEDGE.

W Fawdes.
Captain for
Major,

Temporally. Commanding 30th. Battalion Machine Gun Corps.

Issued by D.R. at 8 p.m.

Copy No. 1. 30th British Division "G".
2. 89th Infantry Brigade.
3. 90th Infantry Brigade.
4. Commanding Officer.
5. O.C. "A" Company.
6. " "B" "
7. " "C" "
8. " "D" "
9. Quartermaster.
10. Signalling Officer.
11. War Diary.
12. " "
13. File.
14. Spare.

SECRET. Copy. No. 19.

Amendment to 30th Battalion Machinb Gun Corps Order No. 33.

22nd September, 1918.

Reference para. 3. (b) (7), for N.33.d.95.30. read N.33.b.95.30.

Captain for
Lieut. Colonel,

Commanding 30th Battalion Machine Gun Corps.

SECRET. Copy No. 19.

30th BATTALION MACHINE GUN CORPS ORDER No. 33.

Reference Sheet 28. S.W. 1/20,000. 19th September, 1918.

1. The 30th Battalion Machine Gun Corps will take over the M.G. Defence of the Right Sector of the Corps Front on the night of 20th/21st September, 1918.

2. The Divisional Front will then be held by 32 machine guns in the line, two M.G. Companies being kept in Divisional Reserve.

3. These guns will be divided into two groups, each of 16 guns as follows:-

(a) Right Group. Headquarters T.19.b.9.9. near Right Bde. H.Qrs.

Posts.

(a) T.9.b.1.1. approximately - 4 guns.
(b) T.22.a.5.8. " - 4 guns.
(c) T.10.d.7.4. " - 2 guns.
(d) T.17.a.25.45. " - 2 guns.
(e) T.12.b.1.1. " - 2 guns.
(f) T.18.b.8.8. " - 2 guns.

(a and b Posts - each of 4 guns - will probably be sub-divided at an early date into 4 posts of 2 guns sited to cover that position of the NEUVE EGLISE LINE in the Right Brigade Area).

(b) Left Group. Headquarters N.31.a.6.7. with Left Brigade Headquarters
Forward H.Q. N.33.d.7.1.

Posts.

(1) T.6.b.7.1. approximately - 2 guns.
(2) T.11.a.9.8. " - 2 guns.
(3) T.4.a.9.7. " - 2 guns.
(4) N.35.a.1.7. " - 2 guns.
(5) T.3.d.6.6. " - 2 guns.
(6) T.3.b.9.9. " - 2 guns.
(7) N.33.d.95.30. " - 2 guns.
(8) N.27.d.5.2. " - 2 guns.

4. "B" Company, 30th Battalion M.G.C. will form the Right Group.
Commander. Major Ingram.

"D" Company, 30th Battalion M.G.C. will form the Left Group.
Commander. Major MacKay.

5. On the night 19/20th September, 1918 the following guns of "D" Company will be withdrawn from their present positions and will relieve the guns of "B" Company as shown in attached Appendix "A". Subsequent to relief, "B" Company will concentrate in the vicinity of Left Group Headquarters in the NEUVE EGLISE LINE and will remain there until the night 20/21st. Completion of moves will be reported to 30th Battalion M.G.C. Headquarters by the code phrase "A.B. 984 received"

6. On the night 20/21st September, 1918, "B" Company 30th Bn. M.G.C. will take over the positions of the Right Group - as stated in para. 3a of these orders - from the 36th Battalion M.G.C.
Guides of the 36th Battalion M.G.C. will meet teams and limbers of "B" Company 30th Battalion M.G.C. at 8-30 p.m. 20/21st September at the junction of the railway and road at T.3.b.2.1.
Completion of relief will be notified to O.C. 30th Battalion M.G.C. by the code phrase "S.C. 148 received".

7. The command of the Machine Guns in the Right Sector of the Corps Front will pass to O.C. 30th Battn. M.G.C. on completion of relief.

8. Details as to S.O.S. Lines will be issued shortly. Until these are issued the present S.O.S. Lines of guns will be adhered to.

9. Reconnaissance of the positions of the 36th Battalion M.G.C. to be taken over will be made by Officers of B. Coy 30th Battalion M.G.C on the 19th and 20th September.

10. All further details of relief will be arranged direct between Group and Company Commanders concerned.

11. ACKNOWLEDGE.

[signature]

Lieut. Colonel,
Commanding 30th Battalion Machine Gun Corps.

Copy No. 1.) 2.) Battalion Headquarters.
3. 30th British Division "G"
4. " " " "Q"
5. 21st Infantry Brigade.
6. 89th Infantry Brigade.
7. 90th Infantry Brigade.
8. Xth Corps M.G.O.
9. 36th Battalion M.G.C.
10. 34th Battalion M.G.C.
11. C.R.A.
12. C.R.E.
13. O.C. "A" Company 30th Bn. M.G.C.
14. "B" " " "
15. "C" " " "
16. "D" " " "
17. O.C. Divisional Signal Coy.
18.) 19.) War Diary.
20. File.
21. Spare.

Original

Confidential

Vol 8

War Diary

of

30th Battalion Machine Gun Corps

for the

Month of October 1918

Volume 6

1-31 October, 1918.

Instructions regarding War Diaries and Intelligence Summaries are contained in F. S. Regs., Part II. and the Staff Manual respectively. Title pages will be prepared in manuscript.

WAR DIARY
or
INTELLIGENCE SUMMARY.
(Erase heading not required.)

Army Form C. 2118.

Place	Date	Hour	Summary of Events and Information	Remarks and references to Appendices
MESSINES.	1/10/18.		Battalion H.Q's moved up to Advanced H.Q's at MESSINES, and Advanced H.Q's were to move to KORTEWILD. This move was afterwards cancelled. Situation unchanged and fairly quiet. "B" Company relieved a Company of the 41st Bn. M.G. Corps and took up positions by 10.00, on the East side of YPRES - COMINES Canal. The 30th Division took over the 41st Divisional front from WERVICQ to COMINES.	
WYTSCHAETE.	2/10/18.		Battalion H.Q's moved to WYTSCHAETE on account of heavy shelling of MESSINES, a report centre being left behind which closed at 06.00 the next day. "A" & "C" Companies were relieved by the 14th Bn. M.G. Corps. "A" Company concentrated at P.19.c. West of HOUTHEM, "C" Company moved into reserve and were billeted at OOSTTAVERNE. 14th Division relieved 30th Division on the West side of YPRES - COMINES Canal	Appendid. 1.
	3/10/18.		Whilst on the road to Battalion Headquarters Captain A.F. Craig and Lieut. T.H. Parkin were severely wounded by shell fire near HOUTHEM.	
	4/10/18.		Captain Craig died at 04.15. and Lieut Parkin at 15.45.	
	5/10/18.		"A" Company moved into the line and took up positions to cover the 89th Brigade Front. "B" Company after relief by "D" Company of the 14th Bn. M.G. Corps, took up positions to cover the front of the 21st Brigade in accordance with Amendment to 30th Bn. M.G.COrps Warning Order No. 40. A draft of 15 O.R's joined the Battalion and were posted to "B" & "C" Companies. Lieut. J.G. Duncan, M.C. joined the Battalion.	Appendix 2. & 2a.
	6/10/18.		Situation unchanged.	
	7/10/18.		Situation still unchanged. Lieut. B.M. Rumbold and Lieut. W.S. Woods joined the Bn. and were posted to "A" Company.	
	8/10/18.		Situation unchanged.	
	9/10/18.		Major Ingram, Lieut. Pascoe and Lieut. Home were evacuated gassed, owing to gas shelling on HOUTHEM, during the night 8th/9th inst. Lieut. R.G. Foster, Lieut. G.A. Pemberton, Lieut. A. McAdie and 2nd Lieut. E.G. Brown joined the Battalion. Lieut. McAdie, Lieut. Foster, & Lieut. Pemberton were posted to "D" Company, 2nd Lieut. Brown to "B" Company.	
	10/10/18.		The Machine Gun Defence of the Divisional front was organised into one Group, consisting of 2 Sub-groups, "A" & "C" Companies under Major J.F.A. Swanston	Appendix 3. & 4.
	11/10/18.		1 N.C.O. and 35 O.R's joined the Battalion and were posted to "B" & "D" Companies. Situation unchanged.	
	12/10/18.		All guns were moved into barrage positions at dusk, in readiness for the operation detailed in Appendix 5. Major J.F.A. Swanston and 2nd Lieut. Billington were gassed and evacuated. Major O.M. Parker took command of Right Group and Lieut. J.F. Roberts, M.C. took command of "C" Company.	Appendix 5. & 5a.

D. D. & L., London, E.C. (10340) Wt W5300/P713 750,000 3/18 E 2688 Forms/C2118/16.

Army Form C. 2118.

Instructions regarding War Diaries and Intelligence Summaries are contained in F. S. Regs., Part II. and the Staff Manual respectively. Title pages will be prepared in manuscript.

WAR DIARY
or
INTELLIGENCE SUMMARY.
(Erase heading not required.)

Place	Date	Hour	Summary of Events and Information	Remarks and references to Appendices
WYTSCHAETE.	13/10/18.		Situation unchanged.	
	14/10/18.		At 05.35 the 30th Division attacked with the object of capturing the objective, Railway in in 28/P.30.c. & b. - Q.25.a. REEKE Village inclusive road junction Q.17.d.1.2. The attack was supported by a machine gun barrage provided by all the machine guns in the Battalion. At 09.30 all objectives were reported to have been gained. "A" & "D" Companies moved forward to consolidate positions. (See Appendix 5.) At 12.00 patrols had been pushed forward towards the R. LYS and into WERVICQ. The following Officers joined the Battalion Captain H.C. Wollaston, 2nd Lieut. W.A. Radcliffe and Lieut. J.R. Powell and were posted to "B" Company. 2nd Lieut. A.H. Morris was posted to "C" Company. At draft of 20 O.R's joined the Bn. and were posted to "A", "B", "C" & "D" Companies.	
	15/10/18.		Infantry started crossing the LYS. "D" Company was relieved by a Company of the 14th Bn. M.G. Corps and moved into billets in the OOSTTAVERNE Area. "B" Company moved into billets in the same area. The following Officers joined the Battalion Lieut. S.W. Nuttall (posted to "D" Company), Lieut. D.H. Neale (posted to "A" Company). A draft of 20 O.R's joined the Bn.	APPENDIX 6.
HOLLEBEKE. Sheet. 28.	16/10/18.		1 Section of "A" Company moved forward in close support of 2/15th London Regt. the remaining sections moved up close to the R. LYS. Infantry moved forward to a line in the neighbourhood of PAUL BUCQ. During the night "C" Company relieved "A" Company 34th Division, covering ground from Q.17.c.2.1. as far as JOB FARM, Q.12.d.9.8. Battalion Headquarters moved from WYTSCHAETE to HOLLEBEKE Area (P.7.a.) "B" & "D" Companies moved into area P.7. and P.8. "A" & "C" Companies were formed into one Group under Major O.M. Parker, for the defence of the Divisional front. The following Officers joined the Battalion Lieut. J.O.N. McKenna, (posted to "B" Company) and 2nd Lieut. H.E. Pickering (posted to "C" Company.)	Appendix 7.
	17/10/18.		The advance was continued. "A" & "C" Companies moved forward in close support of the Infantry. 90th Infantry Brigade occupied high ground in the neighbourhood of BOUSBECQUE. Battalion Headquarters moved forward to Q.15.a. Major Parker moved his Group Headquarters to BOUSBECQUE CHATEAU.	Appendix 8.
RONCQ. Sheet 28.	18/10/18.		90th Infantry Brigade supported by "A" & "C" Companies continued the advance and reached the line STERHOEK - PRESHOEK - KNOCK. "A" & "C" Companies went into billets in 29/X.6.c. and HOOGOORT. Battalion Headquarters moved to Factory at RONCQ. "B" & "D" Companies started from HOLLEBEKE at dawn and reached RONCQ area about 13.00.	
	19/10/18.		The advance continued, "A" & "C" Companies remaining in support of 90th Infantry Brigade. The line at 23.55 ran, T.19.b. along road to TOMBROEK, thence T.8.c. & b. "A" Company moved into billets for the night near LE COMPAS. "C" Company remained at AELBEKE.	

D. D. & L., London, E.C.
(10340) Wt W5300/P713 750,000 3/18 E 2688 Forms/C2118/16.

Instructions regarding War Diaries and Intelligence Summaries are contained in F. S. Regs., Part II. and the Staff Manual respectively. Title pages will be prepared in manuscript.

WAR DIARY
or
INTELLIGENCE SUMMARY.
(Erase heading not required.)

Army Form C. 2118.

Place	Date	Hour	Summary of Events and Information	Remarks and references to Appendices
CROISE.	20/10/18.		Battalion Headquarters moved to CROISE and "B" & "D" Companies to area near CROISE. The 21st Infantry Brigade took over front on left of 90th Brigade and the advance continued; "A" Company in support to 90th Brigade, "C" Company in support to 21st Brigade. Group Headquarter under Major Parker ceased to exist as such and Major Parker rejoined Battalion Headquarters at CROISE. The following Officers joined the Battalion, Lieut. J.G. Frater, Lieut. C.R. Norman (posted to "D" Company) and 2nd Lieut. R.A. Hudson (posted to "A" Company).	
STERHOEK. (Sheet 29.)	21/10/18.		Infantry patrols reached the R. L'ESCAUT. Enemy opposition considerably increased. Battalion H.Q's moved to the CHATEAU at STERHOEK. The advance during the day was closely supported by "A" & "C" Companies.	
MEULEKEN.	22/10/18.		Battalion Headquarters moved to MEULEKEN. Attempts to cross the L'ESCAUT failed, owing to heavy M.G. fire and the difficulty of finding a way through the marsh on the Right bank. Our M.G's harassed occupied areas during the day. "A" & "C" Companies each had one section in close support to the Infantry, the remaining three sections in each case, being in billets near their Company Headquarters in COYGHEM and ST GENOIS, respectively.	
	23/10/18.		~~Situation~~ Situation unchanged. 41st Division reported to have advanced on the left. "C" Company H.Q's were moved to U.14.c.8.3. owing to shelling of ST. GENOIS.	
	24/10/18.		"B" & "D" Companies moved to billets in ROLLEGHEM. Situation unchanged. Lieut. J.R. Strong was transferred from "D" to "B" Company. Lieut. E.N. Dempster was transferred from "B" to "A" Company. A draft of 10 O.R's joined the Battalion.	
	25/10/18.		Situation unchanged.	
	26/10/18.		The 30th Division took over the front of the 34th Division by extending its front to the left. "A" & "C" Companies continued to cover the front of their respective Brigades, and new positions were taken up by 21.00 for this purpose. Captain H.C. Wollaston appointed Second in Command of "B" Company from 19-10-18. Captain. C.H. Tresham appointed to the Command of "C" Company from 24-10-18. Lieut. J.F. Roberts, M.C. appointed Second in Command of "C" Company from the 12-10-18. Lieut. P.S. Greenwell appointed Second in Command of "A" Company from 25-10-18.	Appendix 9 & 9a.
	27/10/18.		The Divisional front was shortened resulting in the withdrawal of the 89th Infantry Brigade, the 21st Infantry Brigade took over the whole of the front. "A" Company was withdrawn from the line and came into reserve with Company H.Q's at COYGHEM. "C" Company disposed its guns so as to cover the whole Divisional front.	Appendix 10 & 10a.

D. D. & L., London, E.C.
(10340) Wt W5300/P713 750,000 3/18 E 2688 Forms/C2118/16.

Instructions regarding War Diaries and Intelligence Summaries are contained in F. S. Regs., Part II. and the Staff Manual respectively. Title pages will be prepared in manuscript.

WAR DIARY
or
INTELLIGENCE SUMMARY.
(Erase heading not required.)

Army Form C. 2118.

Place	Date	Hour	Summary of Events and Information	Remarks and references to Appendices
MEULEKEN	28/10/18.		Situation unchanged.	
	29/10/18.		Situation unchanged. Recreational training was carried out by "B" & "D" Companies and included a Rugby Football match. Headquarters & "B" Company V "D" Company.	
	30/10/18.		Situation unchanged. Lieut. C.E. Elford was transferred from "A" Company to "B" Company from this date. Lieut. J.R. Powell was transferred from "B" to "A" Company from this date.	
ROLLEGHEM.	31/10/18.		Battalion Headquarters moved to ROLLEGHEM. Situation unchanged.	
			For Strength see Appendix 11.	Appendix 11.

[signature] Lieut. Colonel,

Commanding 30th Battalion Machine Gun Corps.

D. D. & L., London, E.C. (10340) Wt W5300/P713 750,000 3/18 E 2688 Forms/C2118/16.

Appendix Confidential

Appendix
to
War Diary
of
30th Battalion Machine Gun Corps
For the month of October 1918

Volume 6. 1-31 Oct. 1918.

APPENDIX I

SECRET. Copy No. 14

30th BATTALION MACHINE GUN CORPS ORDER No. 39.

2nd October, 1918.

1. The Divisional Front held by the 21st Infantry Brigade runs approximately as follows, P.35.d.0.4. - P.34.a.central - P.34.b.0.9. - P.29.d.5.0. - P.24.b.8.8. 14th Division (41st Infantry Brigade) on the right of the 21st Infantry Brigade holds the line COMINES - WARNETON Railway from P.35.d.0.4. to S.W., 35th Division (104th Infantry Brigade) on the left of the 21st Infantry Brigade holding approximately the line P.24.b.8.8. - Q.19.d.2.4. - Q.15.c.0.0. The line then runs N.E. to GHELUWE.

2. At 7 a.m. to-day the 35th and 41st Divisions attacked in the direction of MENIN with the object of capturing the TERHAND Line from Q.17. central - Q.12 central - K.36.
The intention of the Divisional Commander is to make good the line of the River LYS from V.4.a. to P.35.b. as soon as possible. He also intends to advance our line through WERVICQ to the line of the LYS in P.36.a. and b. - Q.31.a. - Q.25.d. and Q.26.c. as opportunity offers, aided by the effect of the operations further East.

3. (a) "B" Company 30th Bn. M.G. Corps is holding the line in conjunction with the 21st Infantry Brigade.
(b) "A" Company 30th Bn. M.G. Corps is located near HOUTHEN and will be prepared in case of necessity ... either,

(i) To reinforce the line held by the 21st Infantry Brigade
(ii) to support a counter attack made to recapture this line.

O.C. "A" Company will reconnoitre this line, and also the routes to it, in conjunction with O.C. "B" Company.

(c) "D" Company 30th Bn. M.G. Corps at present at OOSTTAVERNE will be prepared to occupy a defensive position on the line P.25.c. & b. - P.20.d. - P.21.b.
(d) "C" Company at OOSTTAVERNE is in Divisional Reserve.

4. Special arrangements will be made by O.C. "B" Company to bring a concentration of fire of all available guns on the WERVICQ and the Northern & Western exits from it, if required.

5. Battalion Headquarters are located at O.19.d.2.8.

6. ACKNOWLEDGE.

[signature]

Lieut. Colonel,

Commanding 30th Battalion Machine Gun Corps.

Issued by D.R. at 10.5 p.m.

Copy No. 1. Battalion Headquarters.
2. " "
3. 30th British Division "G".
4. " " " "Q".
5. 21st Infantry Brigade.
6. 89th " "
7. 90th " "
8. M.G.O. Xth Corps.
9. O.C. "A" Company.
10. O.C. "B" Company.

Copy No. 11. O.C. "C" Company.
12. O.C. "D" "
13. Quartermaster.
14. 14th Bn. M.G. Corps.
15. 41st Bn. M.G. Corps.
16. War Diary.
17. " "
18. File.
19. Spare.
20. "

APPENDIX 2(a)

SECRET. VR/G/447.

AMENDMENT TO 30th BATTALION MACHINE GUN CORPS WARNING ORDER No. 40.

5th October, 1918.

1. The operation mentioned in the above order is postponed.

2. After relief by a Company of the 14th Bn. M.G. Corps, "B" Company, 30th Bn. M.G. Corps will dispose its guns to cover the front of the 21st Infantry Brigade, which runs P.30.c.0.3. - P.30.b.1.7. - P.24.d.0.7. - BLOKSTRAAT CABT., Q.13.c.0.7. - Q.13.a.7.0. Move to be complete by 12 midnight, and to be notified to Battalion Headquarters.

3. "A" Company, 30th Bn. M.G. Corps will move into the line and will take up positions to cover the front of the 89th Infantry Brigade, running from Q.13.a.7.0. to Q.8.c.5.6.
Positions are to be occupied before 12 midnight, completion to be notified to Battalion Headquarters.
O.C. "A" Company will get into touch with the 89th Inf. Bde., (Headquarters at P.14.b.4.5.) and will carry out task allotted by the G.O.C. as far as possible.

4. O's. C. "A" & "B" Companies will forward as early as possible the map locations and main lines of fire of their guns, to Battalion Headquarters.

5. The remaining two Companies ("C" & "D") 30th Bn. M.G. Corps will remain in their present location, OOSTTAVERNE, and will be in Divisional Reserve.

6. ACKNOWLEDGE.

W Hawkes
Captain for
Lieut. Colonel,
Commanding 30th Battalion Machine Gun Corps.

Copies to all recipients of 30th Battalion Machine Gun Corps Warning Order No. 40.

APPENDIX 2(a)

SECRET. VR/G/447.

AMENDMENT TO 30th BATTALION MACHINE GUN CORPS WARNING ORDER No. 40.

5th October, 1918.

1. The operation mentioned in the above order is postponed.

2. After relief by a Company of the 14th Bn. M.G. Corps, "B" Company, 30th Bn. M.G. Corps will dispose its guns to cover the front of the 21st Infantry Brigade, which runs P.30.c.0.3. - P.30.b.1.7. - P.24.d.0.7. - BLOKSTRAAT CABT., Q.13.c.0.7. - Q.13.a.7.0. Move to be complete by 12 midnight, and to be notified to Battalion Headquarters.

3. "A" Company, 30th Bn. M.G. Corps will move into the line and will take up positions to cover the front of the 89th Infantry Brigade, running from Q.13.a.7.0. to Q.8.c.5.6.
Positions are to be occupied before 12 midnight, completion to be notified to Battalion Headquarters.
O.C. "A" Company will get into touch with the 89th Inf. Bde., (Headquarters at P.14.b.4.5.) and will carry out task allotted by the G.O.C. as far as possible.

4. O's. C. "A" & "B" Companies will forward as early as possible the map locations and main linesof fire of their guns, to Battalion Headquarters.

5. The remaining two Companies ("C" & "D") 30th Bn. M.G. Corps will remain in their present location, OOSTTAVERNE, and will be in Divisional Reserve.

6. ACKNOWLEDGE.

W.P. Hawkes

Captain for
Lieut. Colonel,

Commanding 30th Battalion Machine Gun Corps.

Copies to all recipients of 30th Battalion Machine Gun Corps Warning Order No. 40.

APPENDIX 3

SECRET. Copy No. 9

30th BATTALION MACHINE GUN CORPS ORDER No. 41.

9th October, 1918.

1. "B" Company, 30th Bn. M.G. Corps will be relieved in the Right Sector of the Divisional Front to-night 9th/10th October, by "C" Company, 30th Bn. M.G. Corps, relief to be complete by 12 midnight.

2. O.C. "C" Company will proceed forthwith to "B" Company Headquarters, and all details of relief will be arranged between "B" & "C" Company Commanders.

3. The Command of the Machine Gun Group covering the Divisional Front will pass to Major J.F.A. Swanston, who will report to and keep in touch with the G.O.C. 89th Infantry Brigade, (Headquarters P.20.d.3.8.)

4. After relief, "B" Company will march back to the billets vacated by "C" Company near OOSTTAVERNE, and will be in Divisional Reserve.

5. Completion of relief will be notified to this Office by the code phrase "VR/G/31 noted".

6. ACKNOWLEDGE.

W.J. Fowles

Captain for
Lieut. Colonel,

Commanding 30th Battalion Machine Gun Corps.

Issued by D.R. at 1830.

Copy No. 1. Battalion Headquarters.
2. 30th British Division "G".
3. 89th Infantry Brigade.
4. O.C. "A" Company.
5. O.C. "B" "
6. O.C. "C" "
7. O.C. "D" "
8. 14th Bn. M.G. Corps.
9. War Diary.
10. " "
11. File.
12. Spare.

SECRET. Copy No. 14

30th BATTALION MACHINE GUN CORPS ORDER No. 42.

Reference Sheet 28. S.E. 1/20,000

10th October, 1918.

1. Reference 30th Bn. M.G. Corps Order No. 40. The Machine Gun Defence of the Divisional Front will be organised forthwith into one Group.

Group Commander - Major J.F.A. Swanston.

He will keep in touch with and arrange to carry out the wishes of the G.O.C. 89th Infantry Brigade.

2. The Machine Gun Group will be divided into two Sub-groups, viz:-

Left Sub-group - "A" Company, 30th Bn. M.G. Corps.

Right Sub-group - "C" Company, 30th Bn. M.G. Corps

Sub-group Headquarters will be notified later.

3. (a) The guns of the Right Sub-group will be disposed to cover the front line running from P.30.c.1.2. to P.24.d.3.2. and to defend the HOUTHEM - TENBRIELEN Defence Line from P.29.d.central (Approx) to P.21.b.7.7. (Approx)

(b) The guns of the Left Sub-group will be disposed to cover the front line running from P.24.d.3.2. to Q.8.c.5.6. and to defend the HOUTHEM - TENBRIELEN Defence Line from P.21.b.7.7. (Approx) to P.17.a.3.2.

The necessary reconnaissances and re-distribution of guns will be carried out forthwith.

The tracings issued to Company Commanders herewith indicate the area in which each Sub-group will operate.

4. "D" Company, 30th Bn. M.G. Corps will be prepared to reinforce the guns in the HOUTHEM - TENBRIELEN Defence Line from P.20.d.3.2. to Q.17.a.central.

5. Barrage lines for all guns, both front and rear, will be laid out

6. ACKNOWLEDGE.

J.G. Robert

Lieut. Colonel,

Commanding 30th Battalion Machine Gun Corps.

Issued by D.R. at

Copy No. 1.) Battalion Headquarters.
2.)
3. 30th British Division "G".
4. 21st Infantry Brigade.
5. 89th Infantry Brigade.
6. 90th Infantry Brigade.
7. 14th Bn. M.G. Corps.
8. 34th Bn. M.G. Corps.
9. O.C. "A" Company.

Copy No. 10. O.C. "B" Company.
11. " "C" "
12. " "D" "
13.) War Diary.
14.)
15. File.
16. Spare.

APPENDIX 5a

SECRET. Copy No. 16

30th BATTALION MACHINE GUN CORPS ORDER No. 43.

Reference Sheet. 28. S.E. 1/20,000.

11th October, 1918.

1. 30th Bn. M.G. Corps Warning Order No. 40 is cancelled and the following order substituted.

2. On a day and at an hour to be notified later, the 30th Division will attack and capture the objective marked on Appendix "A" attached. The attack will be made by the 21st Inf. Bde. on the Right (Headquarters at P.20.d.4.5.) and by the 90th Inf. Bde. on the Left (Headquarters at TRALEE FARM, P.14.b.4.4.). Boundaries between Brigades are shown on Appendix "A".

3. The attack will be supported by the 30th Bn. M.G. Corps and by one Company of the 14th Bn. M.G. Corps. The 30th Bn. M.G. Corps will be divided into two groups as follows:-

Right Group. Commander - Major ~~J.E.A. Swanston~~, Major O.M. Parker.
Headquarters with 21st Inf. Bde. at P.20.d.4.5.
Composition - "B", "C", & "D" Coys, 30th Bn. M.G.C.

Left Group. Commander - Major A.C. Thorn.
Headquarters with H.Q's 2/14 London Regt., AMERICA, P.12.d.
Composition - "A" Coy, 30th Bn. M.G. Corps.

Assembly Area, Q.7.c.

The Company of the 14th Bn. M.G. Corps will form a separate Group under arrangements which will be made by O.C. 14th Bn. M.G. Corps

4. The Right Group and the Group of the 14th Bn. M.G. Corps, will fire a barrage as laid down in Barrage Organisation Scheme, Appendix "B", attached.

"D" Company, 30th Bn. M.G. Corps will also, on the capture of the objective by the 21st Inf. Bde., consolidate the captured area by pushing forward one section to each of the general areas marked on Appendix "A".

The O.C. "D" Company will push forward a patrol at H plus 45 minutes to discover whether the Infantry Objective has been gained, and as soon as he receives information that the ground has been taken, will forthwith move his Sections to their positions of consolidation without any further orders.

He will report to the Group Commander immediately those positions have been consolidated.

5. As soon as the 90th Infantry Brigade have captured their objective, the Left Group Commander will consolidate the captured area by pushing forward his Sections to the general areas marked on Appendix "A".

He will obtain information as to the capture of the objective from the Os' C. the two attacking Infantry Battalions, Headquarters of both of which will be at AMERICA, P.12.d. He will immediately report to 90th Inf. Bde. and through 90th Bde. to Bn. H.Q's. that the Machine Gun consolidation has taken place.

6. On completion of the operation "B" & "C" Companies will be in Divisional Reserve.

7. Battalion Headquarters will remain at their present location.

8. ACKNOWLEDGE.

Lieut. Colonel,

Commanding 30th Battalion Machine Gun Corps.

Issued by D.R. at

Copy No. 1.) Battalion Headquarters.
2.)
3. 30th British Division "G".
4. 21st Infantry Brigade.
5. 89th Infantry Brigade.
6. 90th Infantry Brigade.
7. 14th Bn. M.G. Corps.
8. 34th Bn. M.G. Corps.
9. O.C. "A" Company.
10. " "B" "
11. " "C" "
12. " "D" "
13. Major J.F.A. Swanston.
14. Signal Officer.
15.) War Diary.
16.)
17. File.
18.) Spare.
19.)

30th Battalion Machine Gun Corps.

Copies of messages of appreciation received in connection with Operation carried out August, 21st. 1918.

30th Division, No. G/395. (Wire).

Total captures to-day in this morning's successful attack AAA 2 Officers 107 other ranks 3 Machine Guns AAA All objectives on DRANOUTRE SPUR captured and consolidated including a fair amount of wiring AAA Added to all concerned.

30th Division, No. G/397. (Wire).

Following received begins Xth Corps, please convey to General Williams and 30th Division my congratulations on successful operation last night AAA It was an operation very well planned and carried out, General Plumer ends.

30th Division, No. G/264/406.

The G.O.C. wishes to place on record his appreciation of the gallantry, drive and soldierly conduct of all ranks in to-days action. All three Infantry Brigades were involved and may well be proud of their prowess. The Divisional Artillery as always upheld their high reputation; the M.G. Battalion ably assisted and must have caused many casualties to the enemy; the R.E. and Pioneers were both of great assistance to the Infantry and worked well. The work of clearing the wounded reflects great credit on all ranks of the Field Ambulances.

(Signed). P. Beame.

21-8-18. General Staff, 30th Division.

A SHORT HISTORY OF THE PART PLAYED BY THE 30th BATTALION MACHINE GUN CORPS IN THE CAPTURE OF THE DRANOUTRE RIDGE AND THE ADVANCE OF AUGUST/SEPTEMBER, 1918.

---------------------o---------------------

It being necessary to have a "jumping off" place for the impending British attack on MT KEMMEL, the 30th Division which was holding the line on MTS VIDAIGNE, ROUGE and SCHERPENBERG, was ordered to capture DRANOUTRE RIDGE in August, 1918. Lieut. Colonel H.G.V. Roberts, M.C. Commanding the 30th Battalion Machine Gun Corps made his dispositions as follows:-
"A" Group under Major A.C. Thorn, 30th Bn. M.G. Corps composed of Nos. 1 & 2 Sub-groups under Captain C.H. Tresham and Lieut. L.M. Merricks both 30th Bn. M.G. Corps respectively.
"B" Group under Major H. Leah, 35th Bn. M.G. Corps composed of Nos. 3 & 4 Sub-groups
"C" Group under Major O.M. Parker, 30th Bn. M.G. Corps composed of Nos. 5 & 6 Sub-groups under Captain Denny, 35th M.G. Corps and Captain P.G. Walsh, 30th Bn. M.G. Corps.

"A" Group consisting of 36 guns of the 30th Bn. was located on the forward slopes of MTS. ROUGE and VIDAIGNE, "B" consisting of 4 guns of the 35th Bn, on MT ROUGE and South of SCHERPENBERG, and "C" consisting of 16 guns of the 30th Bn. and 16 guns of the 35th Bn, on the Eastern slopes of ROUGE and south of SCHERPENBERG. The guns of the 36th Bn. and 8 guns of the 41st, firing from positions they already held in the line, co-operated in the scheme making a total of 148 guns.

The 35th Bn. and "A" Company, 30th Bn. being in reserve, moved up into position during the night 19/20th August and by 10 p.m. on the 20th all arrangements were complete. Starting at 2-5 a.m. on the 21st a barrage of seven minutes duration was put down on the enemy lines between KEMMEL and DRANOUTRE. At 2-12 a.m. it lifted to the neighbourhood of SWINDON and ceased forty minutes later. The attack was completelysuccessful and the Infantry easily gained all their objectives and captured over 100 prisoners and 3 machine guns.

An S.O.S. Call was answered at dawn and the guns remained in position throughout the day. During the night of the 21st/22nd the enemy counter attacked four times but was repulsed on each occasion. The following night the guns were withdrawn and "A" Company returned to the Reserve billet near LANCET FARM and the 35th Bn. returned to TERDEGHEM.

Copies of messages of appreciation received from the Army and Divisional Commanders are attached. Mention must be made of Pte. Weir, "D" Company, 30th Bn. M.G. Corps who, "for great coolness and devotion to duty whilst under heavy shell fire", was awarded the Military Medal.

Despite very heavy shelling the casualties sustained by the Battalion was surprisingly few. Three were killed and twenty-two, including Lieuts. Whiffen, Holloway and Orchard were wounded.

On the 23rd August, Lieut. Colonel Roberts went to England on leave and the command of the Battalion devolved upon Major Parker.

The enemy did not allow "A" Company to enjoy a very peaceful rest. At 1 a.m. on the night 23/24th, the Reserve Billets were shelled with H.E., Gas and Incendiary Shells. The house itself receiving three direct hits, was ablaze in five minutes and a large proportion of the Company's guns, gun equipment and personal property was lost. In endeavouring to save the guns and limbers, Offivers and men lost practically everything they possessed save only what they were actually wearing at the time.

It is noteworthy that, in spite of the Farmyard being stacked with S.A.A. and bombs amongst which shells were continually exploding, no casualties were incurred. Some narrow escapes were however experienced. For example, a limber which C.S.M. Willans was trying to save was struck by a shell andthe Sergeant Major was knocked down but luckily received no serious injury.

During the following week "A" Company relieved "C" in the line. The positions, as far as the Machine Gunners were concerned, then being - "A" Company on MT ROUGE, "B" on VIDAIGNE, and "D" on SCHERPENBERG.

On Thursday, August, 29th numerous large fires were observed and many explosions were heard behind the enemy's lines, and it soon became evident that he had no intention of waiting to be driven off KEMMEL, but intended making a general withdrawal on our front. Patrols of our Infantry out during the following night reported that the enemy had withdrawn but had left many strong posts held by machine guns. During the following day strong patrols encountered stubborn resistance from some of these "nests" particularly in the neighbourhood of MONT DE LILLE. By 11-30 p.m, however, the Division had made a general advance of more than a mile and was in touch with the 36th Division which was advancing on our right.

As a result of a conference held on MT NOIR at 8-30 a.m. on Saturday, August, 31st, Major Parker concentrated "A" Company and 2 Sections of "D" at WESTOUTRE and 2 Sections of "B" on MT VIDAIGNE. The remaining Sections of "B" under Lieuts. Home and Grigson co-operated with the 89th Brigade on the Divisional Right Flank and the remaining 2 Sections of "D" under Lieuts. Jones and Woodhead were affiliated to the 21st Brigade on the left. On September, 1st. Lieuts. Home and Grigson with two Sections of "B" Company were ordered to prepare to support the 89th Brigade in an attack upon NEUVE EGLISE. At a conference held at the Brigade Headquarters at 2-30 p.m. on the 2nd. September, it was decided that the attack should be launched at 6-30 p.m. and that one Section should provide covering fire whilst the other advanced in close support of the Infantry. Lieut. Home accordingly placed his guns on the high ground some 2,000 yards west of the village with a view to providing covering fire. Lieut. Grigson advanced with "C" Company 7/8 Inniskilling Fusiliers, but the machine gun and trench mortar opposition caused severe casualties amongst the Infantry and they were forced to fall back to a line near STAMPKOTMOLEN about 500 yards north of NEUVE EGLISE. Fresh orders then arrived from Brigade that a second attack would be made at 1-30 a.m. and the village captured at all costs. Lieut. Grigson took two guns with "A" Company, Inniskillings, and sent two under 2nd Lieut. Clark with "C" Company. This time the opposition was not so strong and although machine gun and trench mortar fire was encountered our troops were not seriously impeded. A small party of the enemy appeared near the machine gunners on the road in the middle of the village, but they made good their escape before the guns could be brought into action. Proceeding through the village the gunners dug themselves in about 500 yards East of it, the Infantry occupying a line just in front of them. The guns remained in these positions until 11-30 a.m., on the 3rd. they withdrew according to orders with the Infantry who were being relieved. 2nd Lieut. Lewis with No. 3 Section "B" Company affiliated to the 90th Brigade proceeded to the vicinity of DAYLIGHT CORNER on September, 1st. The following night the London Scottish, with whom he was co-operating were relieved by the 2/15 Londons (Civil Service Rifles) and moving forward with them, he sited his guns on the ridge East of WULVERGHEM. On the night 2/3rd. he was relieved by 2nd Lieut. Weeks who remained in the front line until relieved by "C" Company a week later.
Meanwhile on August, 31st. "C" Company moved up to LOCRE CHATEAU in the 89th Brigade Area. On the march Major W.R. Lewis and Lieut. Trethowan were wounded and as Captain Tresham was away on Leave, the command passed to Lieut. J.F. Roberts, M.C.

On the night of the 1st. orders were received to support the 7/8th Inniskillings in their attack on NEUVE EGLISE. Two Sections with Pack Transport moved up and, after the first attack had failed, remained in action covering a gap of about 700 yards between the Inniskillings and South Lancs.

During the night 2/3rdbeing ordered to move to the Divisional Left Flank, the Company withdrew to the neighbourhood of BODGER FARM, North of LA DOUVE RIVER with a view to working round to the 21st Brigade Front. On the morning of the 3rd. the Company moved off as a mobile column and formed its Headquarters at BEAVER HALL CAMP, communications being established with the 21st Brigade. The same day orders were received from Battalion Headquarters to relieve "A" Company who were holding the main line of resistance running due South of BEAVER HALL CAMP. "A" Company then took "C"s place in the forward area and supporting the 21st Brigade advanced to beyond DAYLIGHT CORNER. Lieut. March sited his Battery of 8 guns along a line South of FRENCHMAN'S FARM and in doing so he came in for a good deal of sniping from very close range. Fortunately he was not hit. The other Battery under Lieut. Elford was sited about 700 yards North East of WULVERGHEM. This Batteries remained in position during the next six days and assisted the Infantry by carrying out harassing fire on enemy roads, tracks and machine gun locations. A barrage was fired on the night of the 6th, which helped the Infantry to close a gap in the line North East of WULVERGHEM. During this action Sgt. Markwick and Pte. Asling distinguished themselves by showing great coolness and contempt for their own personal safety under very heavy shell fire. They have since both been awarded the Military Medal. During the night 9/10th the Company was relieved and withdrew to WESTOUTRE. Before marching off, the Transport Lines in the DOUVE VALLEY near DAYLIGHT CORNER were heavily shelled with Gas causing many casualties amongst the Drivers and Mules. There is no doubt the casualties would have been much heavier but for the pluck and coolness of L/Cpl. Harris who although suffering from Gas poisoning immediately encouraged his Drivers to stand by the Mules and personally remained with them until the following morning when by orders of the Medical Officer, he was sent to hospital. For this action L/Cpl. Harris has been awarded the Military Medal.

The splendid weather of the previous ten days then gave way to exceedingly heavy and cold rainstorms and both sides, being more or less hampered by the mud, settled down to stationary warfare again, with the enemy holding MESSINES RIDGE.

SECRET & URGENT. Copy No. 15

30th BATTALION MACHINE GUN CORPS ORDER No. 36.

26th September, 1918.

1. Reference 30th Bn. M.G. Corps Order No. 35. ZERO lines for Batteries will be laid out on the night of 26/27th.

2. Groups and Sub-groups will take up positions and will be ready to fire as detailed in 30th Bn. M.G. Corps Order No. 35 before midnight on 27th.
Completion of move to be notified to Bn. Headquarters by the code phrase "S.C. 921 received".

3. Advanced Battalion Headquarters will move to positions as detailed in 30th Bn. M.G. Corps Order No. 35. by 8 p.m. on 27th inst. Completion of move to be notified to Battalion Headquarters by the code phrase "B.M. 432 received".

4. Battalion Headquarters will open at N.31.a.6.7. at 8 p.m on 27th, and will close at present location at the same hour.

5. Signal Communications as detailed in 30th Bn. M.G. Corps Order No. 35. will come into use at 8 p.m. 27th inst.

6. ACKNOWLEDGE.

[signature]

Lieut. Colonel,

Commanding 30th Battalion Machine Gun Corps.

Issued by D.R. at. 12 noon

Copy No. 1. Battalion Headquarters.
2. " "
3. 30th British Division "G".
4. 89th Infantry Brigade.
5. 90th Infantry Brigade.
6. O.C. "B" Company.
7. O.C. "C" "
8. O.C. "D" "
9. Major C.M. Parker.
10. " D. MacKay.
11. " C.D. Ingram.
12. Signal Officer 30th Bn. M.G. Corps.
13. File.
14. War Diary.
15. " "
16. Spare.

Copy No. 1. Commanding Officer.
2. -do-
3. 30th British Division "G".
4. 30th British Division "Q".
5. C.R.A.
6. C.R.E.
7. 21st Infantry Brigade.
8. 89th Infantry Brigade.
9. 90th Infantry Brigade.
10. A.D.M.S.
11. O.C. "A" Company 30th Bn. M.G. Corps.
12. "B" " " " " "
13. "C" " " " " "
14. "D" " " " " "
15. O.C. Divisional Signal Coy.
16. 30th Bn. M.G. Corps Signal Officer.
17. Lieut. R.J. Wheatley.
18. Xth Corps M.G.O.
19. 34th Battalion M.G.Corps.
20. 31st Battalion M.G. Corps.
21. File.
22.}
23.} War Diary.
24. Spare.

SECRET. Copy No. 22.

30th BATTALION MACHINE GUN CORPS ORDER No. 35.

Reference Sheets.1/10,000 HELL FARM.
1/40,000 Sheet 28. 23rd September, 1918.

1. The Divisional Boundaries from a night to be notified later, will be as follows:-

North Boundary. N.28.d.3.7. - POND FARM - KRUISSTRAAT CABARET - TORREKEN CORNER - O.21.central - O.22.c.9.4.

South Boundary. T.16.c.6.6. - FORT EBERLE - LE ROSSIGNOL - U.8.c.6.6. - thence along DOUVE RIVER.

The Divisional Front is held by two Brigades. From the above date the Inter-Brigade Boundary is MESSINES - WULVERGHEM ROAD.

2. On "J" day and at "H" hour, strong fighting patrols will push forward with a view to capturing certain enemy posts. Should the enemy withdraw it is intended that the Division should advance its line to the Eastern Slopes of the MESSINES RIDGE.
Should strong hostile opposition be met the above mentioned patrols will not push on, but at a later hour strong fighting patrols will again be sent out with the same object.

3. The advance of these patrols will be covered by the fire of 3 Machine Gun Companies of the 30th Bn. M.G. Corps divided into two Groups as follows:-

RIGHT GROUP. (Supporting Right Infantry Brigade)

Commander. Major Ingram. Headquarters to be notified later.
Composition "B" Company 30th Bn. M.G.C. 16 guns. Batteries on forward slopes of Hill 63 in Squares T.12.d. and T.18.b.

LEFT GROUP. (Supporting Left Infantry Brigade).

Commander. Major MacKay. Headquarters near SOUTH MIDLAND FARM.
Composition. "C" & "D" Companies 30th Bn. M.G.C. 32 guns. Batteries on Forward Slopes of high ground in T.6.

Group Commanders will arrange to cover the Infantry advance with direct fire and to bring their fire to bear on localities as desired by the G.O.C. the Infantry Brigade which they are supporting.
It must be clearly understood that every opportunity will be taken of engaging visible targets with direct fire and so supporting the advance.
When the MESSINES RIDGE has been occupied by our troops, "B" and "D" Companies will advance their Batteries about 1,000 yards so as to be able to cover with long range fire the objective of the Division, shown on map already issued to O.C. Companies.
"C" Company will be prepared to concentrate at short notice with a view to moving forward on Pack and Limber Transport as Forward Company.

4. "A" Company, 30th Bn. M.G. Corps, on "J" - 1 night will concentrate between DAYLIGHT CORNER - AIRCRAFT FARM with transport (pack and limber) as FORWARD Company. This Company will, on receipt of orders, be prepared to move forward to consolidate the MESSINES RIDGE, with two sections supporting each Infantry Brigade. Company Headquarters will then be established on the MESSINES - WULVERGHEM Road in the vicinity of MOULIN DE L'HOSPICE, MESSINES.

5. On "J" - 1 night Battalion Headquarters will be at N.31.a.6.7. ADVANCED Battalion Headquarters and Report Centre will be established at T.3.b.60.98., near ARMOUR FARM, on "J"- 1 night.

6. Communications. Signal Officer 30th Bn. M.G. Corps, will arrange for communication as follows:-

Runner Service:-

Forward Company Headquarters, Objective MOULIN DE L'HOSPICE.
to
LEFT GROUP Headquarters, near SOUTH MIDLAND FARM.
to
ADVANCED Battalion Headquarters, near ARMOUR Farm.
to
Battalion Headquarters, N.31.a.6.7.

RIGHT GROUP Headquarters to ADVANCED Battalion Headquarters.

In addition he will take steps to ensure that visual stations are maintained from FORWARD COMPANY to RIGHT and LEFT GROUP.
RIGHT GROUP to ADVANCED Bn. Headquarters.
LEFT GROUP to ADVANCED Bn. Headquarters.

Telephone Communication with direct lines will be established and maintained between,
RIGHT GROUP HEADQUARTERS and ADVANCED BATTALION HEADQUARTERS.
LEFT " " " " "

Telephone Communication through Division will be maintained between Advanced Bn. Headquarters and Battalion Headquarters.

7. Lieut. R.J. Wheatley and Battalion Scouts will be at LEFT GROUP Headquarters. Lieut. Wheatley will be responsible for reporting through LEFT GROUP Commander the earliest moment at which it is possible for "A" Company to advance alongthe MESSINES - WULVERGHEM ROAD to MOULIN DE L'HOSPICE, and the time at which our Infantry gain the MESSINES RIDGE.

8. The principles laid down in this Office VR/G/326 and VR/G/326/1 will be adhered to.

9. Bridges for limbers, suitable for laying across demolished roads, will be dumped in WULVERGHEM at a location which will be notified to all concerned indue course. Limbers of Forward Company will use those as required.

10. Advanced Battalion Headquarters are responsible for maintaining liaison with both attacking Brigades and for ensuring that the Brigadiers' wishes as to M.G. Fire are carried out as far as possible.

11. ACKNOWLEDGE.

[signature]

Lieut. Colonel,

Commanding 30th Battalion Machine Gun Corps.

Issued by D.R. at 9.45pm

SECRET & URGENT.

30th BATTALION MACHINE GUN CORPS ORDER No. 57.

Reference Sheet 28 Belgium and France 28th September, 1918.

1. 41st Division has reached the ECLUSE No. 4 on the YPRES - COMINES Canal (P.20.c.9.2.) and at dawn on the 29th. will continue its advance S.E. on the Eastern side of the Canal.

2. The Boundaries of the front allotted to the 30th Division are as follows:-
Northern Boundary From the present Boundary to O.21.central thence to ECLUSE No. 4. P.13.a.

Southern Boundary From the present Boundary to U.10.a.0.7. through cross roads in O.35.c.7.3. inclusive, and thence to YPRES - COMINES CANAL at P.20.c.9.2.
Inter-Brigade Boundary From present Boundary U.34.b.6.5. in a straight line to Bridge at HOUTHEM P.19.b.8.9.

The Task allotted to the 30th Division is to clear the enemy of the area between the MESSINES RIDGE and the YPRES - COMINES CANAL enclosed between the above Boundaries. The Infantry will advance from the present line which runs approximately N.W. and S.E. through MOULIN DE L'HOSPICE at 5-30 a.m. 29th inst.

3. "A" Company, 30th Bn. M.G. Corps which is located at present near SOUTH MIDLAND FARM will act as Forward Company and will support the advance of each Brigade with two Sections.
"A" Company will move forward from their present position when information is received that the MESSINES RIDGE is in our possession. O.C. "A" Company will take the necessary steps to ensure by observation or patrols that immediately information of the capture of the MESSINES RIDGE reaches him. O.C. "A" Company will issue all further orders and will notify Battalion Headquarter through Left Group Commander of the location and road of advance of his Headquarters. He will ensure that the closest liaison is maintained with the Infantry and that situation reports are forwarded to Battalion through Left Group at least every 1½ hours from 5-30 a.m.
Lieut. Wheatley and the Battalion Scouts are placed forthwith at the disposal of O.C. "A" Company.
Care must be taken that our own troops both on the Eastern and Western sides of the YPRES - COMINES CANAL are not endangered by our Machine Gun Fire.

4. Left Group Commander will arrange for a Report Centre to be established as early as possible on the road near MOULIN DE L'HOSPICE U.2.a. and is responsible that all communications received from O.C. "A" Company are forwarded without delay to Advanced Bn. Headquarters.

5. "B", "C" and "D" Companies will be in Divisional Reserve from 6-30 a.m. 29th inst. and will be prepared to move forward at short notice if required.

6. ACKNOWLEDGE.

[signature]
Lieut. Colonel,
Commanding 30th Battalion Machine Gun Corps.

Issued by D.R. at midnight

Copy No. 1. Battalion Headquarters.
2. Advanced Battalion Headquarters.
3. O.C. "A" Company.
4. O.C. "B" Company.
5. O.C. "D" Company.
6. O.C. "C" Company.
7. Left Group Commander, 30th Bn. M.G. Corps.
8. Lieut. R.J.Wheatley.
9. Major J.F.A. Swanston.
10. 30th Division "G".
11. 21st Infantry Bde.
12. 89th Infantry Bde.
13. 90th Infantry Bde.
14. War Diary.
15 " "
16. Spare.

APPENDIX "A".

Moves of Machine Guns on night of 19/20th September, 1918, in Left Sector of Xth Corps Front.

-------------------------0-------------------------

(1) 2 guns "D" Company from STINKING FARM. T.7.a.	to T.3.d.6.6. approx.	in relief of	2 guns "B" Company.
(2) 2 guns "D" Company from N.35.a.1.7. approx.	to N.27.d.5.2. approx.	" " "	4 guns "B" Company.
(3) 2 guns "D" Company from Forward Reserve.	to T.3.b.9.9. approx.	" " "	2 guns "B" Company.
(4) 2 guns "D" Company from Forward Reserve.	to N.33.d.95.30. approx	" " "	4 guns "B" Company.

Guns and Teams of "B" Company after relief concentrate near SUB-GROUP Headquarters in NEUVE EGLISE LINE.

APPENDIX A

Consolidation Areas. Shown. Thus.-

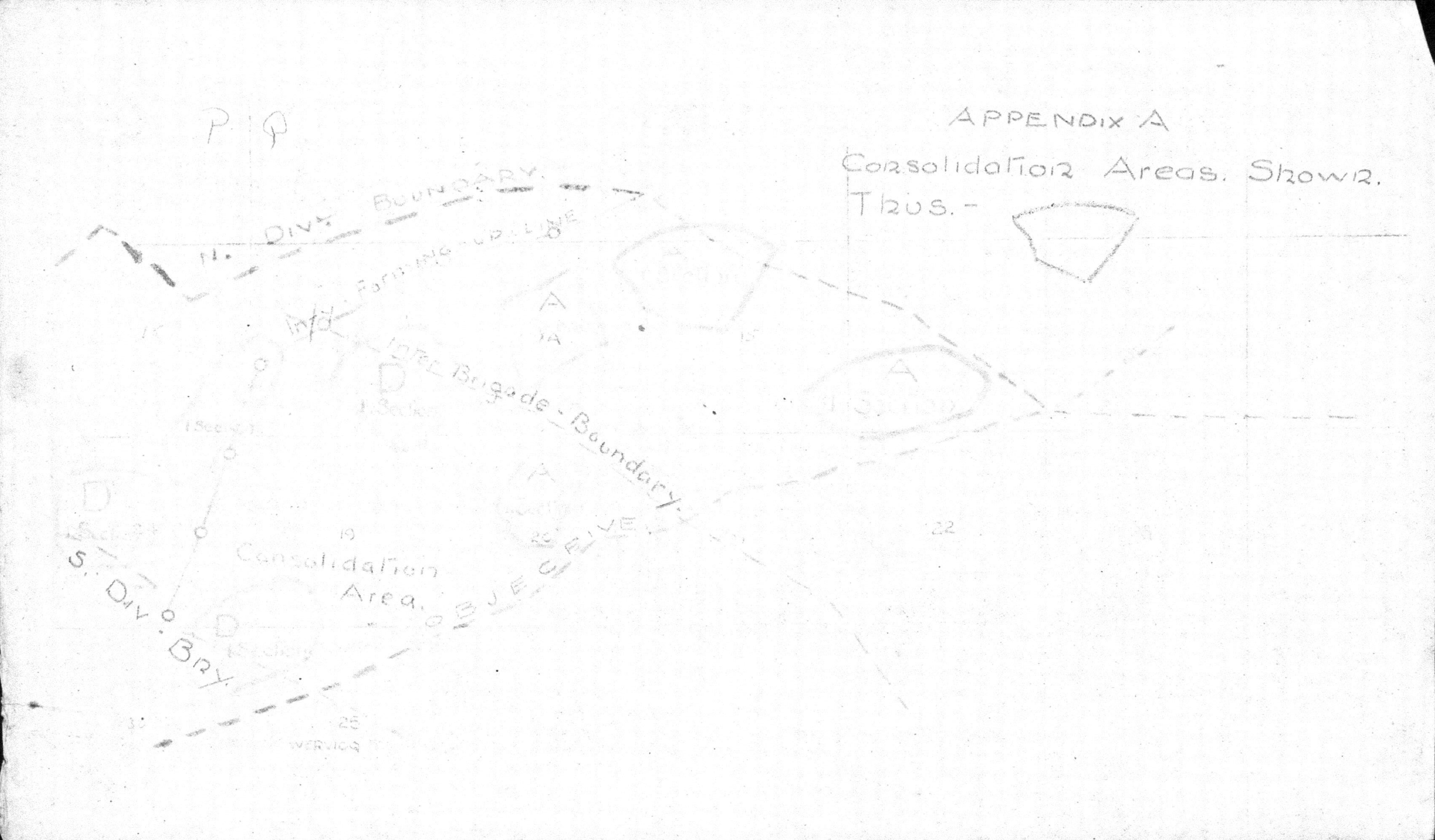

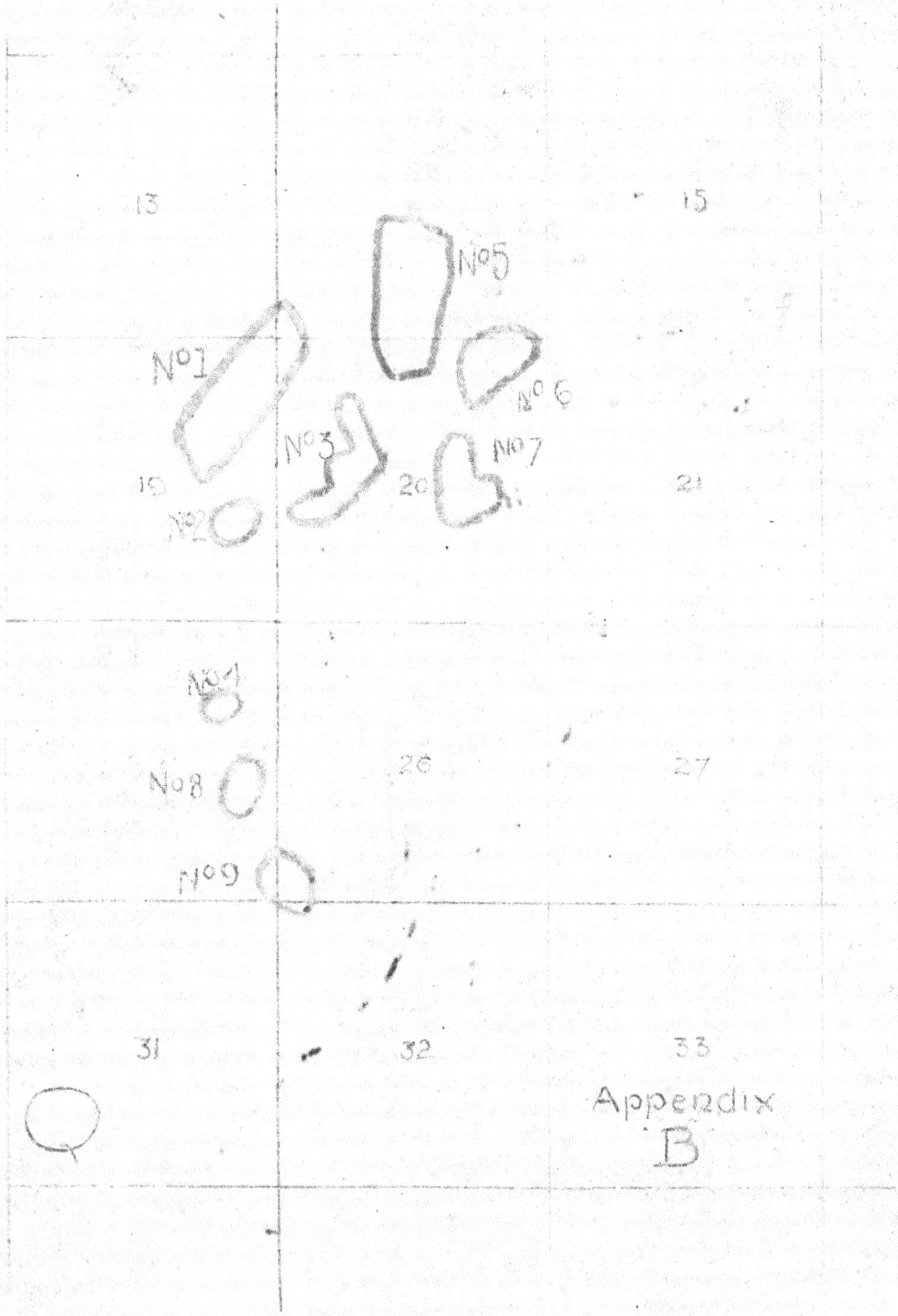
13
15
No5
No1
No6
No3
No7
19
20
21
No2
No4
No8
26
27
No9
31
32
33
Appendix
B

APPENDIX "F".

BARRAGE ORGANIZATION SCHEME TO 30th BATTALION MACHINE GUN CORPS ORDER NO. 43.

RIGHT GROUP.

"B" Company.	1 Battery 8 guns. Location P.18.a.2.4.	1st Task.	Area No. 5.	H – 3 to H plus 5.	Intense.
		2nd Task.	Area No. 6.	H plus 5 to H plus 10.	Intense.
		3rd Task.	Area No. 7.	H plus 10 to H plus 20.	Intense.
	1 Battery 8 guns. Location P.18.a.40.45.	1st Task.	Area No. 6.	H – 3 to H plus 10.	Intense.
		2nd Task.	Area No. 7.	H plus 10 to H plus 20.	Intense.
"D" Company.	1 Battery 8 guns. Location not yet decided.	Task.	Area No. 3.	H – 3 to H plus 10.	Intense.
	1 Battery 8 guns. Location not yet decided.	Task.	Area No. 4.	H – 3 to H plus 10.	Intense.
"C" Company.	2 Batteries 12 guns. Locations P.29.b.20.98. P.23.d.8.2.	1st Task.	Area No. 1.	H – 3 to H plus 5.	Intense.
		2nd Task.	Area No. 8.	H plus 5 to H plus 18.	Intense.
	1 Battery. 4 guns. Location P.24.c.20.65.	1st Task.	Area No. 2	H – 3 to H plus 8.	Intense.
		2nd Task.	Area No. 8.	H plus 8 to H plus 18.	Intense.

Group of 14th Bn. Machine Gun Corps,

16 guns. Concentration on Bridge at Q.25.d.9.2. (Area No. 9.) From H – 3 to H plus 120 minutes. Rate of Fire. 75 R.P.M.

Group and Company Commanders are responsible that safety clearance over our Infantry is maintained. Infantry Jumping-off line is marked on Appendix "A", and rate of advance is 100 yards every 2 minutes.

VR/G/506

SECRET & VERY URGENT.

ADDENDUM TO 30th BATTALION MACHINE GUN CORPS ORDER No. 43.

12th October, 1918.

1. All guns will be moved at dusk tonight, 12th/13th October, into their positions in readiness for the operation stated in 30th Bn. M.G. Corps Order No. 43, moves to be complete by midnight.
Completion of move of Left Group will be notified to Bn. H.Q's by the code phrase "A.F. B.122 forwarded".
Completion of move of Right Group will be notified to Bn. H.Q's by the code phrase "VR/22 received".

2. Headquarters of both Groups will remain in their present location until 6 p.m. to-morrow, 13th inst, when Left Group H.Q's will move to AMERICA, P.12.d., and Right Group will move to 21st Brigade H.Q's, P.20.d.4.5.

3. Communication.
Communication from Left Group to Bn. H.Q's will be made through Right Group.
Left Group Commander is responsible that an efficient runner service is maintained between his H.Q's and Right Group H.Q's.
Right Group Commander is responsible in a similar way for the runner service from his H.Q's to Bn. H.Q's.

4. (a) Major C.M. Parker will be in Command of the Right Group in place of Major J.F.A. Swanston.
(b) Lieut. J.F. Roberts will be in Command of "C" Company.

5. ACKNOWLEDGE.

W J Hawkes
Captain for
Lieut. Colonel,
Commanding 30th Battalion Machine Gun Corps.

Copies to all recipients of 30th Bn. M.G. Corps Order No. 43.

SECRET. APPENDIX 6 Copy No. 12

WARNING
30th BATTALION MACHINE GUN CORPS/ORDER No. 44.

14th October, 1918.

1. "D" Company, 30th Bn. M.G. Corps will be relieved in the Right Sector of the line by a Company of the 14th Bn. M.G. Corps on the night 15th/16th October, relief to be complete by midnight.

2. The O.C. the Company of the 14th Bn. M.G. Corps will proceed to Right Group Headquarters, P.20.d.4.5. to-morrow morning, October, 15th where a guide will be provided to conduct him to Headquarters, "D" Company, 30th Bn. M.G. Corps.

3. All details of relief will be arranged direct between the Company Commanders concerned.

4. On relief, "D" Company will march to billets in the PILLEGREM FARM Area, O.24.b. and d, and P.19.a. and c. O.C. "D" Company will send a party to obtain accommodation and to meet the Company on its arrival.

5. Completion of relief will be notified to Battalion Headquarters by the code phrase "Extra leave vacancy required urgent".

6. ACKNOWLEDGE.

A.J. Hawkes Capt
for Lieut. Colonel,
Commanding 30th Battalion Machine Gun Corps.

Issued by D.R. at

Copy No. 1. Battalion Headquarters.
2. 30th British Division "G".
3. 21st Infantry Brigade.
4. 90th Infantry Brigade.
5. O.C. "A" Company.
6. O.C. "B" "
7. O.C. "C" "
8. O.C. "D" "
9. Major O.M. Parker.
10. 14th Bn. M.G. Corps.
11. War Diary.
12. " "
13. File.
14. Spare.

APPENDIX 7

13.

SECRET.

30th BATTALION MACHINE GUN CORPS ORDER NO. 45.

15th October, 1918.

1. On the night 16th/17th October, "C" Company, 30th Bn. M.G. Corps, will relieve "A" Company, 34th Bn. M.G. Corps in the line.

2. A guide of the 34th Bn. will meet O.C. "C" Company at AMERICA cross roads, P.12.b.0.8. at 08.00 to-morrow October, 16th. to conduct him to Headquarters, "A" Company, 34th Bn., located at Q.9.a.05.30.

3. The ground to be covered by this Company extends from the present Northern Divisional Boundary, Q.17.c.2.1. (approx) as far East as JOB FARM, Q.12.d.9.8.

4. The relief will be completed by 12 midnight and completion reported to the Battalion Report Centre, P.7.b.1.1. (for transmission to Bn. Headquarters) by the code phrase "Hasten reply BM.2". Command to pass on completion of relief.

5. From completion of the relief, the Divisional front will be held by 2 Machine Gun Companies ("A" & "C" Companies), organised into one Group.

Group Commander. Major C.M. Parker.

Headquarters with 90th Infantry Brigade, location to be notified later.

6. Communication. "C" Company will communicate to Battalion Headquarters through the Report Centre, a line to which will be laid as early as possible.

7. ACKNOWLEDGE.

W.J. Lawlin Capt
for Lieut. Colonel,

Commanding 30th Battalion Machine Gun Corps.

Issued at

Copy No. 1. Battalion Headquarters.
2. 30th British Division "G".
3. 21st Infantry Brigade.
4. 90th Infantry Brigade.
5. Major C.M. Parker.
6. O.C. "A" Company.
7. O.C. "B" "
8. O.C. "C" "
9. O.C. "D" "
10. 34th Bn. M.G. Corps.
11. 14th Bn. M.G. Corps.
12. Signal Officer.
13.) War Diary.
14.)
15. File.
16. Spare.

APPENDIX 8

SECRET & VERY URGENT. Copy No. 8

30th BATTALION MACHINE GUN CORPS ORDER No. 46.

Reference Sheet. 28. S.E. 1/20,000

15th October, 1918.

1. The enemy are retreating. The 30th Division will advance and maintain touch with the enemy.

2. The Southern Divisional Boundary BOUSBECQUE to RONCQ both inclusive. Northern Divisional Boundary after relief of 34th Division on night 16/17th, Bridge at R.14.b.9.0. - RECKEM (R.29.a.) - CROISE (R.36.a.) all inclusive.

3. 90th Brigade will cross R. LYS between BOUSBECQUE and MALPLAQUET and advance with first objective high ground in W.4.a. - R.31.a. Patrols will push forward inadvance of this line and keep close touch with the enemy. 34th Division previous to relief are operating to establish line from LE MALPLAQUET South and East of HALLUIN to LE CORNET at R.22.a.

4. "A" Company, 30th Bn. M.G. Corps will move forward in close support of the 90th Brigade., main line of advance BOUSBECQUE - RONCQ Road.
Two Sections will move in advance and two in support, Company Headquarters only move when necessary and then will move along the BOUSBECQUE - RONCQ Road and will display M.G. Flag conspicuously. If Company Headquarters move they will leave a Report Centre at their present location through which messages can be forwarded. Group Headquarters will be with 90th Brigade from 10-30 a.m. to-morrow, 16th inst. Major O.M. Parker Group Commander will establish telephonic communication with Battalion Headquarters immediately on arrival.

5. "C" Company, 30th Bn. M.G. Corps will be prepared to move at 1 hours notice from 10 a.m. 16th inst. with pack and fighting limbers. They will be required to support the advance N. of a line drawn from LE MALPLAQUET Q.30. to MONT d'HALLUIN X.3.b. to the NORTHERN DIVISIONAL BOUNDARY, when the 30th Division takes over this front from the 34th Division and will take over this area by 10 p.m. 16th inst. Further instructions will be issued with regard to the action of this Company in due course.

6. Fighting Limbers and Pack Transport of "A" Company under Lieut. Stephens will report to "A" Company Headquarters at 8 a.m. 16th inst.

7. Pontoon Bridge is being made at BOUSBECQUE by C.R.E.

8. Major Parker, O.C. "A" Company, Lieut. Stephens and O.C. "C" Company to acknowledge.

[signature]

Lieut. Colonel,
Commanding 30th Battalion Machine Gun Corps.

Copy No. 1. 30th British Division "G".
2. 90th Infantry Brigade.
3. O.C. A Company.
4. O.C. C Company.
5. Major O.M. Parker.
6. Lieut. Stephens, T.O. "A" Company.
7. War Diary.
8. " "
9. Spare.
10. File.

SECRET.

APPENDIX 9

Copy No. 13.

30th BATTALION MACHINE GUN CORPS ORDER No. 49.

26th October, 1918.

1. 30th Division will take over the front of the 34th Division to-night 26th/27th October.
21st Infantry Brigade will do this by extending their front to the left and relieving the 102nd Infantry Brigade of the 34th Division.
After the readjustment the Northern Divisional Boundary will run:-

N.29.central - O.28.central - AUTRYVE,(V.9.a.9.0.) - ESCANAFFLES (excl.) - CAPON, (V.24.c.) incl.

2. To-night 26th/27th October, 89th Infantry Brigade will take over from the 21st Infantry Brigade as far North as U.24.a.5.2.
The new inter-brigade boundary will then run:-

U.9.c.5.0. - U.15.b.6.3. - U.17.d.3.3. - U.24.a.5.2. - U.24.d.central - QUESNOY and CELLES, both inclus. to Right Brigade

3. "A" Company will continue to cover the front of CURRIES Group, with two Sections in line and two in reserve.
"C" Company will continue to cover the front of GOODMANS Group, with two Sections in line and two in reserve.
O's. C. "A" & "C" Companies will ensure that they have guns sited to effectively cover all approaches to the river. Positions will be reconnoitred for the Reserve guns on the high ground in U.10., V.16., and U.21.
"B" & "D" Companies will remain in Reserve.

4. Company Commanders will ensure that any new positions required are taken up by 9 p.m. to-night.

5. ACKNOWLEDGE.

W J Fawdes Capt
for Lieut. Colonel,
Commanding 30th Battalion Machine Gun Corps.

Issued at

Copy No. 1. Battalion Headquarters.
2. 30th British Division "G".
3. 30th British Division "A" & "Q".
4. 21st Infantry Brigade.
5. 89th Infantry Brigade.
6. 90th Infantry Brigade.
7. 34th Bn. M.G. Corps.
8. 41st Bn. M.G. Corps.
9. O.C. "A" Company.
10. "B" "
11. "C" "
12. "D" "
13. War Diary.
14. " "
15. File.
16. Spare.

SECRET. APPENDIX 10 Copy No. 15

30th BATTALION MACHINE GUN CORPS ORDER No. 50.

Reference Sheet 29. 1/40,000

26th October, 1918.

1. On the night 27th/28th October, the portion of the Divisional front held by the 89th Infantry Brigade will be taken over by a Brigade of the 14th Division, and "A" Company, 30th Bn. M.G. Corps, will be relieved by a M.G. Company of the 14th Bn. M.G. Corps.
Further particulars of this relief will be issued as soon as known.
On the same night, the Divisional front will be extended N. East to AVELGHEM, inclus.
The whole of this front will be held by the 21st Infantry Brigade, and by a M.G. Group consisting of "A" & "C" Companies, 30th Bn. M.G. Corps

Group Commander. Major A.C. Thorn.

2. The following will be the dispositions of M.G's :-

Forward Sub-group.("C" Company). Sub-Group Commander Captain C.H. Tresham.

1 Section in general vicinity	U.18.a.
1 " " " "	V.7.d.
1 " " " "	V.3.c.
1 " " " "	P.33.d.

Of the above Sections, the 2 first named are already in position. Reconnaissance of the remaining two positions will be made on the morning of 27th inst. by Captain C.H. Tresham and Section Officers concerned and the sections will move into position at dusk.
Limbers can cross the COURTRAI - BOSSUYT Canal at O.28.b.4.8.

Rear Sub-group.("A" Company) will occupy positions as follows:-

2 Sections at Farm at U.10.b.
1 Section with 2 guns on either side of LOCK 5, U.12.b.
1 " in P.25.d. or P.31.b.
The special task of this last section is the protection of the left flank.
"A" Company will arrange for the necessary reconnaissance of these positions and will move its Sections at present in reserve to the two last-named positions at dusk.
The remaining two Sections will move to Farm in U.10.b. after relief.

3. Suitable position for Group H.Q's will be reconnoitred in U.3.a., O.32.d. or O.33.c. to-morrow morning. Forward Sub-group Commander will reconnoitre for a suitable H.Q's on E. side of COURTRAI - BOSSUYT Canal.
Battalion Headquarters will remain in its present location.

4. Forward Sub-group Commander will notify completion of moves to Bn. H.Q's by code phrase "Easton reply A.D.2". Rear Sub-group Commander will notify Bn. H.Q's of completion of moves by code phrase "Your B.M. 24 acknowledged".

5. ACKNOWLEDGE.

H. G. Robinson

Lieut. Colonel,
Commanding 30th Battalion Machine Gun Corps.

Copy No. 1. Battalion H.Q's.
2. 30th Brit. Div. "G"
3. " " " "A" & "Q"
4. 21st Infy. Bde.
5. 89th " "
6. 90th " "
7. 14th Bn. M.G.C.
8. 35th Bn. M.G.C.

Copy No. 9. O.C. "A" Company.
10. "B" "
11. "C" "
12. "D" "
13. Major A.C. Thorn.
14. File.
15. War Diary.
16. " "
17. Spare.

APPENDIX (10a)

SECRET. VR/G/613.

AMENDMENT No. 1. TO 30th BATTALION MACHINE GUN CORPS ORDER No.50.

27th October, 1918.

1. That part of 30th Bn. M.G. Corps Order No. 50. concerning the extension of the Divisional Boundary N.E. to AVELGHEM inclus. and the moves in conjunction therewith, are cancelled. The Northern Divisional Boundary runs as follows:-

N.29.central - O.28.central - AUTRYVE (V.9.a.C.0.) - ESCANAFFLES (excl.) - CAPON (V.24.c.) inclus.

The Southern Divisional Boundary runs as follows:-

T.21.d.0.0. - U.24.c.0.0. - U.30.central - V.25.d.9.0.

2. The 21st Infantry Brigade will cover the Divisional front, supported by "C" Company, 30th Bn. M.G. Corps.
The M.G's will remain in their present positions.
"C" Company Headquarters will be established at Farm, U.13.b.4.0.

3. After relief by "C" Company, 14th Bn. M.G. Corps, "A" Company, 30th Bn. M.G. Corps will be accommodated at their present billets at COYGHEM, and will be in close support.

W J Sawdes

Captain for
Lieut. Colonel,

Commanding 30th Battalion Machine Gun Corps.

Copies to all recipients of 30th Battalion Machine Gun Corps Order No. 50.

Killed.		Wounded.		Sick.		Otherwise.		Reinforcements.	
O.	O.R.	O.	O.R.	O.	O.R.	O.	O.R.	O.	O.R.
2.	6.	7.	84.	5.	45.	5.	86.	18.	144.

	O.	O.R.		O.	O.R.
Strength on October 1st.				49.	884.
Struck off Strength	O.	O.R.			
Killed.	2.	6.			
Wounded.	7.	84.			
Sick.	5.	45.			
Otherwise.	5.	86.			
	19.	221.		19	221.
				30.	663.
Reinforcements.	O.	O.R.			
	18.	144.		18.	144.
Strength on October, 31st.				48.	807.

Confidential

Original

829

War Diary

of

30th Battalion Machine Gun Corps

For the month of November, 1918

Volume VI

1–30 Nov. 1918.

Instructions regarding War Diaries and Intelligence Summaries are contained in F. S. Regs., Part II. and the Staff Manual respectively. Title pages will be prepared in manuscript.

WAR DIARY
or
INTELLIGENCE SUMMARY.
(Erase heading not required.)

Army Form C. 2118.

Place	Date	Hour	Summary of Events and Information	Remarks and references to Appendices
ROLLEGHEM.	1st Nov.		The Battalion was in the line on the West bank of the R. SCHELDT, with 2 Companies ("A" & "C") in the line and 2 Companies ("B" & "D") at ROLLEGHEM. "C" Company Headquarters moved to O.35.a.1.1., Sheet, 29.	
	2nd Nov.		Situation unchanged.	
	3rd Nov.		Church Parades were held for "B" & "D" Companies and Bn. H.Q's in ROLLEGHEM. Several inter-Company Football matches were played.	
	4th Nov.		51 Other Ranks joined the Battalion.	
BELLEGHEM.	5th Nov.		Battalion Headquarters moved to BELLEGHEM. "D" Company moved into billets near BELLEGHEM.	
	6th Nov.		"B" Company moved into billets North of ROLLEGHEM. The following temporary appointments were made:- Major G.S. Nelson, M.C. to be Second in Command vice Major O.M. Parker (Hospital), Captain W.J. Fawkes, M.C. to command "D" Company vice Major D.S. MacKay, M.C., D.C.M. (Hospital), Lieut. F.C.T. Woodhead to be 2nd in Command "D" Company vice Captain P.G. Walsh (Hospital), Lieut. J.G. Duncan, M.C. to be Acting Adjutant vice Captain W.J. Fawkes, M.C., Lieut. J.G. Frater to be Assistant Adjutant vice Lieut. J.G. Duncan, M.C.	
	7th Nov.		"B" Company moved into billets in BELLEGHEM. Two sections of "C" Company at LOCK 5. and POLDRIESCH were relieved by two sections of the 29th Bn. M.G. Corps. These two sections of "C" Company moved into reserve near "C" Company Headquarters, which had moved to O.15.d.3.7. (Sheet 29). The right section of "A" Company was relieved by a section of "C" Company. The sections of "A" Company at RUGGE and KAPOEK were relieved by a section of the 31st Bn. M.G. Corps. The whole of "A" Company moved into reserve in billets near "A" Company's Headquarters at P.19.a.4.6.	APPENDIX 1. 1A. & 1B.
	8th Nov.		Situation unchanged.	
HEESTERT	9th Nov.		The enemy having commenced a general retirement, the 89th Infantry Brigade forced the passage of the River ESCAUT. "C" Company Headquarters moved to B.8.d.2.8. "C" Company continued to be insupport of the 89th Infantry Brigade, with two sections in the line and two sections in reserve in the vicinity of Company Head quarters. "A" Company remained at P.19.a.4.6.	APPENDIX 2.
			The Battalion less "A" & "C" Companies moved to HEESTERT.	APPENDIX 3.
WATRIPONT.	10th Nov.		The Battalion less "C" Company moved to WATRIPONT. "C" Company continued to move as Forward Company.	APPENDIX 4.
BRUYERE.	11th Nov.		The Battalion less "C" Company moved to BRUYERE. The two forward sections of "C" Company were withdrawn into reserve. An Armistice between the Allies and Germany having been signed, orders were received to cease fire at 11.00 hours.	" 5.

D. D. & L., London, E.C.
(10340) Wt W5300/P713 750,000 3/18 E 2688 Forms/C2118/16.

Instructions regarding War Diaries and Intelligence Summaries are contained in F. S. Regs., Part II. and the Staff Manual respectively. Title pages will be prepared in manuscript.

WAR DIARY
or
INTELLIGENCE SUMMARY.
(Erase heading not required.)

Army Form C. 2118.

Place	Date	Hour	Summary of Events and Information	Remarks and references to Appendices
BRUYERE.	12th Nov.		Notice that the following Officers had been awarded the MILITARY CROSS received:- 2nd Lieut. W.M. Bain and 2nd Lieut. S.W. Kelty.	
	13th Nov.		Indoor and Outdoor Amusement Committees were formed.	
ELLEZELLES	14th Nov.		Battalion Headquarters moved to ELLEZELLES. "C" Company moved into billets vacated by Battalion Headquarters at BRUYERE.	APPENDIX 6.
RENAIX.	15th Nov.		The Battalion moved to RENAIX.	" 7.
AVELGHEM.	16th Nov.		The Battalion moved to AVELGHEM.	" 8.
LUINGHE (Near MOUSCRON)	17th Nov.		The Battalion moved to LUINGHE.	" 9.
	18th Nov.		Companies held cleaning-up and inspection parades.	
	19th Nov.		A Thanksgiving Service was held in the Cinema for Church of England and Nonconformist Denominations. In the afternoon inter-Company football matches were played. The following reinforcements joined the Battalion, Lieut. R.B. Sparrow (posted to "D" Coy), Lieut. J.E. Sanderson, (posted to "A" Coy), 2nd Lieut. A.M. Davies and 2nd Lieut. W.L. Mawer (posted to "C" Coy), and 47 Other Ranks.	
	20th Nov.		A Thanksgiving Service for Roman Catholics was held in LUINGHE Church. The Commanding Officer interviewed 40 men from each Company. The following inter-Company football match was played:- "A" Coy (1st XI) V "C" Coy (1st XI).	
	21st Nov.		The Education Scheme was started, classes being held for instruction in French, Telegraphy, Mathematics, Electricity, and Elementary Reading and Writing. The Commanding Officer continued interviewing men from each Company.	
	22nd Nov.		Training was carried out by Companies in the morning. Recreational training was carried out each afternoon.	
	23rd Nov.		The Commanding Officer lectured the Battalion on the Demobilisation Scheme. The Battalion Rugby team played a team of the 2nd Bn. S. Lancs. Regt. Result. 2nd Bn. S. Lancs. Regt. 8 Points. Battalion. 6 Points.	
	24th Nov.		Usual training carried out. The following Officers joined the Battalion:- Captain W. Veitch, Lieut. A.H. Bartley (posted to "B" Coy), Lieut. R.W. Burton, M.C. (posted to "C" Coy), Lieut. A.D. Barnetson, and 2nd Lieut. T. Aitken (posted to "A" Company). Subaltern Officers paraded for Boxing Practice. The Battalion Association team played a team of the 89th Brigade Headquarters, our team winning by 3 goals to nil.	
	25th Nov.		The Battalion (less Transport) carried out a route march through STERHOEK - AELBEKE - ROLLEGHEM - LE COMPAS.	
	26th Nov.		Usual training carried out.	

D. D. & L., London, E.C.
(10340) Wt W5300/P713 750,000 3/18 E 2688 Forms/C2118/16.

Army Form C. 2118.

Instructions regarding War Diaries and Intelligence Summaries are contained in F. S. Regs., Part II. and the Staff Manual respectively. Title pages will be prepared in manuscript.

WAR DIARY
or
INTELLIGENCE SUMMARY.

(Erase heading not required.)

Place	Date	Hour	Summary of Events and Information	Remarks and references to Appendices
LUINGHE.	27th Nov.		A Rugby Match was played against 30th Divisional Headquarters, our XV winning easily.	
LA VIGNETTE	28th Nov.		The Battalion moved to LA VIGNETTE, the first stage of its move to STAPLES.	APPENDIX 10.
CROIX AU BOIS	29th "		The Battalion moved to CROIX AU BOIS.	" 11.
BAC ST MAUR	30th Nov.		The Battalion moved to BAC ST MAUR.	" 12.

[signature]

Lieut. Colonel,

Commanding 30th Battalion Machine Gun Corps.

D. D. & L., London, E.C.
(10340) Wt W5300/P715 750,000 3/18 E 2688 Forms/C2118/16.

Confidential

Original

V8

Appendix

for

War Diary

of

30th Battalion Machine Gun Corps

for the month of November 1918

Volume VI

1-30-11-18.

Appendix 1

SECRET. Copy No. 15

30th BATTALION MACHINE GUN CORPS ORDER No. 53.

5th November, 1918.

1. (a) On night 6th/7th November, CURRIES Group will be relieved on front from V.4.a.8.6. to P.30.c.0.0. by 31st Division.
(b) Machine Gun posts of "A" Company
viz 1 Section at RUGGE.
1 " " KAPHOEK

will be relieved on the night 6th/7th by M.G's of the 31st Battalion and subsequent to relief will withdraw into reserve in the Forward Area. Billets to be allotted by Staff Captain, 89th Infantry Brigade. "A" Company will then have 1 Section in the line with 2 guns in V.4.a. and 2 guns in P.33.c., and 3 Sections in Reserve.

2. (a) On night 6th/7th, STEVENS Group will take over front from U.30.c.central to his present right at U.24.d.6.3., additional front being taken over from 41st Brigade, 14th Division. Lieut. Col. Pearson, 2/18th London Regt. (H.Q's, U.6.d.3.5.) will command outposts from U.30.c.central to V. 4.a.8.6. on completion of reliefs on night 6th/7th. Cancelled
(b) O.C. "C" Company will dispose his right section and section now at LOCK 5, to cover additional front and will establish a M.G. post on the S.E. bank of the River ESCAUT between U.30.central and U.24.d.6.3. for the defence of the Infantry posts in this locality. The closest liaison will be maintained by O.C. "C" Company with Lieut. Col. Pearson.

3. At 9 a.m. 7th November, CURRIES GRoup will take over command of the Divisional Forward area and of the outpost troops. "A" & "C" Companies will then form one M.G. Group under Major Tresham, Group Commander, 4 Sections (3 Sections "C" Company and one Section "A" Company) being in the line and the remaining 4 Sections in support in the Forward Area.

4. On night 7th/8th the section of "A" Company in the line will be relieved by the Reserve section "C" Company, and will rejoin the remainder of "A" Company in support.

5. The front from U.30.c.central to V.14.d.0.0. will probably be handed over to the 29th Division on night 7th/8th November, in which case the M.G's of "C" Company in this area will move into Reserve at or near Group Headquarters.

6. Major Tresham will arrange to establish his H.Q's with or near 89th Infantry Brigade Headquarters, which will be at O.23.a.5.3.

7. ACKNOWLEDGE.

W. Hawkes.
Captain for
Lieut. Colonel,
Commanding 30th Battalion Machine Gun Corps.

Copy No. 1. Battalion H.Q's.	Copy No. 10. O.C. "A" Coy.
2. " "	11. O.C. "B" "
3. 30th British Division "G".	12. O.C. "C" "
4. " " " "A".	13. O.C. "D" "
5. 89th Infantry Brigade.	14. Major Tresham.
6. 90th Infantry Brigade.	15. War Diary.
7. 21st Infantry Brigade.	16. " "
8. 31st Bn. M.G. Corps.	17. File.
9. 14th Bn. M.G. Corps.	18. Spare.

SECRET.

IA.

AMENDMENT No. 1. TO 30th BATTALION MACHINE GUN CORPS ORDER No. 53.

30TH BATTALION, MACHINE GUN CORPS. No. KR/G/684 Date 6.11.18

6th November, 1918.

1. Para. 2. (a and b) is cancelled.

2. The dispositions of M.G's at 9 a.m. on the 7th November will therefore be as follows.

One M.G. Group consisting of "A" & "C" Companies under Major Tresham.

"C" Company will be on the right and will dispose its guns as follows:-

2 Sections in the line.
1 Section in support at LOCK 5.
1 Section in Reserve.

"A" Company will be on the left and will dispose its guns as follows:-

1 Section in the line (with 2 guns in V.4.c. and 2 guns in P.33.c.)
3 Sections in Reserve.

3. "A" & "C" Companies to acknowledge.

[signature]
Captain for
Lieut. Colonel,

Commanding 30th Battalion Machine Gun Corps.

Copies to all recipients of 30th Bn. M.G. Corps Order No. 53.

SECRET.

18

30TH BATTALION. MACHINE GUN CORPS. VR/G/691 7-11-18

ADDENDUM TO 30th BATTALION MACHINE GUN CORPS ORDER No. 53.

7th November, 1918.

1. Reference para. 5, Order No. 53, the front from U.30.c.central to V.14.d.0.0. will be taken over by the 29th Division on the night 7th/8th inst.

The two Sections of "C" Company at LOCK 5. and POLDRIESCH will be relieved by two Sections of the 29th Battalion M.G. Corps. Details of relief to be arranged between Company Commanders concerned.

2. Reference para 6, This will be carried out. 89th Infantry Brigade Headquarters will be at 0.16.c.0.9.

Subsequent to relief the two Sections of "C" Company will move into Reserve near "C" Company Headquarters.

Captain for
Lieut. Colonel,
Commanding 30th Battalion Machine Gun Corps.

Copies to all recipients of 30th Battalion Machine Gun Corps Order No. 53.

Appendixe 2

SECRET. VR/G/700.

1. CURRIE'S Group forced passage over River ESCAUT last night and captured prisoners.
Enemy are now retreating.

2. CURRIE'S Group will follow up and pass his Group across river, GOODMANS/and STEVEN'S Groupswill be prepared to move forward at 1 hours notice.
"C" Company, 30th Bn. M.G. Corps will continue to act in support of CURRIE'S Group.
"B" Company will support STEVEN'S Group if necessary and will be prepared to move at 1 hours notice.
"D" Company will support GOODMAN'S Group if necessary.
"A" Company will be in Divisional Reserve and will remain in their present location.

3. C.R.E. is putting a pack animal bridge across river at V.15.a.4.2. as soon as possible and will push on with construction of road bridge at ESCAMAFFLES.

4. STEVEN'S is moving one Battalion to HOEN at once for work under C.R.E. on bridge approaches.

5. ACKNOWLEDGE.

[signature] Duncan
Captain for
Lieut. Colonel,
9-11-18. Commanding 30th Battalion Machine Gun Corps.

Copy No. 1. 30th British Division "G".
2. " " " "A" & "Q".
3. 29th Battalion M.G. Corps.
4. 31st Battalion M.G. Corps.
5. O.C. "A" Company.
6. "B" "
7. "C" "
8. "D" "
9. War Diary.
10. " "
11. File.
12. Spare.

Appendix 3

SECRET. Copy No. 8

30th BATTALION MACHINE GUN CORPS WARNING ORDER No. 55.

9th November, 1918.

1. 30th Machine Gun Battalion less "A" & "C" Companies will move to-day to HEESTERT Area.

2. Order of March will be as follows - Headquarters, "D" Company and rear echelon "C" Company, "B" Company.
Starting point will be junction of roads N.26.c.50.00. Head of column will pass starting point at an hour to be notified later.

3. Route will be LE CHAT CABARET - T.5.b.3.6. - PERKE MOULIN, (C.27.c.) - HOOGESTRAATE - KEMERGROOLEN - HEESTERT.

4. A billeting party consisting of one Officer from Headquarters, "B" and "D" Companies will proceed forthwith to HEESTERT, and arrange to billet their respective units.
These Officers will meet the column, subsequently at C.30.c.2.4. (Windmill).

5. DRESS. Full marching Order. Companies will arrange to carry their own blankets, either on the men or on limbers.

6. Battalion Headquarters will close at BELLEGHEM at an hour to be notified later opening in HEESTERT Area on arrival.

7. ACKNOWLEDGE.

Captain for
Lieut. Colonel,

Commanding 30th Battalion Machine Gun Corps.

Copy No. 1. 30th British Division "G".
2. " " " "A" & "Q".
3. O.C. "A" Company.
4. "B" "
5. "C" "
6. "D" "
7. Lieut. Webster, Bn. H.Q's.
8. War Diary.
9. " "
10. File.

Appendix H

SECRET. Copy No. 7

30th BATTALION MACHINE GUN CORPS ORDER NO. 56.

Ref. TOURNAI Sheet 1/100,000
Sheet 29. 1/40,000.
Sheet 37. 1/40,000.

9th November, 1918.

1. The 29th Division is on a N. & S. line through BAUREAUX. The 31st Division is on a N. & S. line through WITTENTAK with cyclists in RENAIX. CURRIES Group are on Railway line S. of RENAIX.

2. The 30th Division will continue the advance to-morrow 10th inst. The leading troops of CURRIES Group will cross the FRASNES - RENAIX Railway at 09.00 and advance to line of road approximately N. & S. through ELLEZELLES. They will billet on night 10/11th in area between this road and FRASNES - RENAIX railway (RENAIX exclusive), covered by outposts EAST of road. "C" Company, 30th Bn. M.G. Corps will continue to be in support of CURRIES Group.

3. GOODMANS Group will move to billets in area bounded by lines N. & S. through second T. of WATRIPONT and A of ANSEROEUL, exclusive of WATRIPONT (Reference 1/100,000 TOURNAI).

4. STEVENS Group will move to MOEN - HEESTERT - VIERKEERHOEK Area.

5. 7th DRAGOON GUARDS will move to HAUT to-morrow, 10th inst.

6. The order of march on completion of bridge at ESCANAFFLES will be - Divisional Cable Waggon - One Battery 38th Army Bde. R.F.A. - 1st line transport CURRIES Group and remainder of CURRIES Group. All these will be under CURRIES orders.

7. 30th Bn. M.G. Corps less "C" Company will move to-morrow 10th inst. to WATRIPONT. Order of march will be Battalion H.Q's. "D" Company with rear echelon "C" Company, "B" Company, "A" Company. O.C. "D" Company will be responsible for issuing orders for movement of rear echelon "C" Company.

8. Starting point will be road junction at P.31.a.85.55.
Head of column will pass starting point at 08.15.
No distances will be maintained between Companies until the R. ESCAUT has been crossed. Route and billeting arrangements will be notified later.
Dress. Full Marching Order.

9. ACKNOWLEDGE.

[signature]
Captain for
Lieut. Colonel,
Commanding 30th Battalion Machine Gun Corps.

Copy No. 1. 30th British Division "G".
2. " " " "A" & "Q".
3. O.C. "A" Company.
4. " "B" "
5. " "C" "
6. " "D" "
7. War Diary.
8. " "
9. File.
10. Spare.

Appendix 5

SECRET. Copy No. 8

30th BATTALION MACHINE GUN CORPS ORDER No. 57.

10th November, 1918.

1. Enemy were holding North and South line through FLOBECQ about 15.30 to-day with weak rearguard. Divisional Outposts are on North and South line through ELLEZELLES in touch with 31st Division on North but not in touch on South with 29th Division.

2. The 30th Division will continue the advance on 11th inst. CURRIE'S Group will establish outposts on W. bank of R. DENDRE between LES DEUX ACREN (inclusive) and OVERDOULAEGE (inclusive), with bridgehead at LES DEUX ACREN, to secure bridge.

3. "C" Company, 30th Bn. M.G. Corps will continue to be in support to CURRIE'S Group.

4. 30th Bn. M.G. Corps less "C" Company will move to BRUYERE (30/S.24.c.) to-morrow. Order of march will be as follows:-

Battalion Headquarters, "D" Company with rear echelon "C" Company, "A" Company, "B" Company.

O.C. "D" Company to issue necessary move order to Officer in Charge "C" Company (rear echelon).
Starting point will be junction of railway and road at 37/X.20.c.1.4. The head of the column will pass the starting point at 10.30 hours.

5. One Officer and two Other Ranks from each Company will report to Battalion Headquarters at 09.00 hours to-morrow and will act as billeting party for their Companies.
Officers will be mounted and Other Ranks with bicycles.

6. Dress. - Full Marching Order. Company Commanders will ensure that the strictest march discipline is observed.

7. ACKNOWLEDGE.

[signature]
Captain for
Lieut. Colonel,
Commanding 30th Battalion Machine Gun Corps.

Copy No. 1. 30th Division "G".
2. " " "I" & "Q".
3. O.C. "A" Company.
4. " "B" "
5. " "C" "
6. " "D" "
7. War Diary.
8. " "
9. File.
10. Spare.

Appendix 6

SECRET. Copy No. 9

30th BATTALION MACHINE GUN CORPS ORDER No. 58.

13th November, 1918.

1. The following moves will take place to-morrow 14th instant.

Battalion Headquarters will move to ELLEZELLES at 10.00 hours.

"C" Company will move to billets at present occupied by Battalion Headquarters in BRUYÈRE. Move to be complete by 14.00 hours.

2. Battalion Headquarters will close at BRUYÈRE at 10.00 hours and reopen at ELLEZELLES on arrival.

3. ACKNOWLEDGE.

[signature]
Captain for
Lieut. Colonel,

Commanding 30th Battalion Machine Gun Corps.

Copy No. 1. 30th British Division "G".
2. " " " "A" & "Q".
3. O.C. "A" Company.
4. O.C. "B" "
5. O.C. "C" "
6. O.C. "D" "
7. Lieut. C.A. Webster, Bn. H.Q's.
8. War Diary.
9. " "
10. File.

Appendix 7

SECRET. Copy No. 10

30th BATTALION MACHINE GUN CORPS ORDER No. 59.

14th November, 1918.

1. The 30th Bn. M.G. Corps will move to RENAIX to-morrow 15th inst. by route march.

2. Order of march will be as follows:-

   Battalion Headquarters, "B" Company, "A" Company, "D" Company and "C" Company.

3. Starting point will be junction of roads 30/S.29.a.5.6.
   Head of column will pass this point at 10.00 hours.

4. Dress:- Full marching order with blanket on pack, service caps, steel helmet strapped on pack, Box Respirators.

5. Interval of 10[x] will be kept between Companies.

6. An Officer from each Company will report to the head of the column at 09.55 to synchronise watches.

7. One mounted Officer and 8 Other Ranks on bicycles from Battalion Headquarters and each Company will report to Major Nelson at 09.00 hours at Battalion Headquarters, as billeting party for their Company.

8. Battalion Headquarters will close at ELLEZELLES at 10.00 hours and reopen at RENAIX on arrival.

9. ACKNOWLEDGE.

Captain for
Lieut. Col.
Commanding 30th Battalion Machine Gun Corps.

Copy No. 1. 30th British Division "G".
2. " " " "A" & "Q".
3. O.C. "A" Company.
4. O.C. "B" Company.
5. O.C. "C" Company.
6. O.C. "D" Company.
7. Major Nelson.
8. Lieut. Webster, Bn. H.Q's.
9. War Diary.
10. " "
11. File.

appendix 8

SECRET. Copy No. 9

30th BATTALION MACHINE GUN CORPS ORDER No. 60.

Reference Map Sheet. 5. TOURNAI
1/100,000. 15th November, 1918.

1. The 89th Infantry Brigade Group (89th Infantry Brigade, 30th Bn. M.G. Corps, 97th Field Ambulance) will move from present area to HEESTERT - MOEN - ESCANAFFLES area to-morrow, 16th inst.

2. 30th Battalion M.G. Corps will be the head of the column. Order of march will be, Battn. H.Q's, "D" Company, "C" Company, "A" Company, "B" Company.

3. Starting point will be junction of roads 1 mile North of T. in BIEST.

4. Head of the column will pass this point at 07.15 hours.

5. Battalion Transport will march in rear of "B" Company. 2nd Lieut. G.C. Grimshaw will be in charge of the Transport and will make all necessary arrangements with Company Transport Officers.

6. Battalion Headquarters will close at 06.00 hours at RENAIX and reopen on arrival in new area.

7. A billeting party, consisting of 1 mounted Officer and 2 Other Ranks per Company and Battn. H.Q's. will report to Major Nelson at the starting point at 07.00 hours.

8. ACKNOWLEDGE.

[signature]
Captain for
Lieut. Colonel,
Commanding 30th Battalion Machine Gun Corps.

Copy No. 1. 89th Infantry Brigade.
2. O.C. "A" Company.
3. " "B" "
4. " "C" "
5. " "D" "
6. Lieut. J.A. Webster, Battn. H.Q's.
7. Major G.S. Nelson, M.C.
8. Battn. Transport Officer.
9. War Diary.
10. " "
11. File.

Appendix 9

SECRET. Copy No. 11

30th BATTALION MACHINE GUN CORPS ORDER No. 61.

Reference Map Sheet 29. 1/40,000
" " " 5. TOURNAI, 1/100,000. 16th November, 1918.

1. CURRIES Group are moving to-morrow to LUINGNE area. 30th Bn. M.G. Corps will move to this area to-morrow 17th inst.

2. Starting point will be junction of roads 29/V.3.c.8.0. Head of the column will pass this point at 08.45 hours.

2 3. Order of march will be Battalion Headquarters, "C" Company, "A" Company, "B" Company and "D" Company.
O.C. "C" Company will arrange to have personnel of his Company formed up on AUTRYVE - MEERSCHTRAAT road 100^x N.E. of starting point at 08.30 hours.

3. Battalion Transport under the Command of 2nd Lieut. C.C. Grimshaw will march in rear of the Battalion.
This Officer will make necessary arrangements with Transport Officers of "A", "B" & "D" Companies for forming up at starting point. Transport of "B" & "A" Companies will not move till personnel of "D" Company has crossed railway in V.4.a.
"C" Company Transport will be formed up just W. of starting point, on WOFFLESTRAAT Road, and will join the Transport column when ordered by 2nd Lieut. C.C. Grimshaw.

4. Billeting parties of 1 mounted Officer and 2 O.R's on bicycles from each Company and Battn. H.Q's. will report to Major Nelson at the starting point 08.00 hours.
Officers in charge of billeting parties will arrange to meet their respective Companies, on completion of billeting in new area, at 11.30 hours at 29/S.24.c.30.95 (junction of roads in LUINGNE)

5. Battalion Headquarters will close at AVELGHEM at 08.15 hours and reopen on arrival in new area.

6. ACKNOWLEDGE.

J.G. Duncan
Captain for
Lieut. Colonel,
Commanding 30th Battalion Machine Gun Corps.

Copy No. 1. 89th Infantry Brigade.
2. O.C. "A" Company.
3. "B" "
4. "C" "
5. "D" "
6. Battalion Headquarters.
7. " "
8. Lieut. C.A. Webster.
9. Quartermaster.
10. Battn. Transport Officer, (2nd Lieut. C.C. Grimshaw).
11. War Diary.
12. " "
13. File.

Appendix 10

SECRET. **Copy No.** 15.

30th BATTALION MACHINE GUN CORPS ORDER No. 68.

Reference Maps. TOURNAI.) 1/100,000.
HAZEBROUCK.)
Sheet 36. 1/40,000.

27th November, 1918.

1. The 30th Bn. M.G. Corps will march with the 89th Infantry Brigade Group to LA VIGNETTE, near LINSELLES to-morrow, 28th inst., where it will stage one night.

2. (a) The starting point will be the Railway crossing, the head of the column will pass this point at 10.30 hours.

(b) Order of March. H.Q's, "B", "C", "A", "D" Companies Bn. H.Q's will form up outside "C" Company's billets, with Headquarter transport immediately in rear.

Companies will form up in rear of Bn. H.Q's, in the order of march. Transport will march with Companies.

Supply wagons will march in rear of "D" Company Transport.

3. Road intervals. Intervals of 200 yards will be kept between Companies. No transport is to be on the LUINGNE CHURCH - RAILWAY CROSSING Road until 89th Infantry Brigade Headquarters have passed Battalion Headquarters.

4. An Officer from each Company will synchronise watches at Orderly Room at 09.15 hours.

5. Blankets. Companies will dump 1 blanket per man at Quartermasters Stores at 7.30 a.m. All blankets of Bn. H.Q's will be dumped at the same time and place. Blankets will be rolled in bundles of 10, securely tied and labelled.

6. Dress. Full marching order, less steel helmets and box respirators which will be carried in limbers. Jerkins carried in packs.

7. Companies will be prepared to supply a hot meal to the men en route. "B" & "C" Companies will prepare a midday meal for Bn. H.Q. personnel.

8. On arrival in billets, Company Commanders will send two runners each to Bn. H.Q's, with their location. A billeting list will be rendered as early as possible after arrival.

9. ACKNOWLEDGE.

W.J. Sanders

Captain for
Lieut. Colonel,
Commanding 30th Battalion Machine Gun Corps.

Copy.No. 1. 30th Division "G".
2. " " "Q".
3. 89th Infy. Bde.
4. Bn. Headquarters.
5. " "
6. O.C. "A" Company.
7. O.C. "B" "
8. O.C. "C" "
9. O.C. "D" "
10. O.C. "H.Q" "
11. Quartermaster.
12. Medical Officer.
13. File.
14.)
15.) War Diary.
16. Spare.

Appendix 11.

SECRET.

COPY No.

30th BATTALION MACHINE GUN CORPS ORDER No. [illegible].

Reference Map. HAZEBROUCK, 1/100,000. 28th November, 1918.

1. The 30th Bn. M.G. Corps will move to CROIX AU BOIS to-morrow, 29th November.

2. Order of March. Bn. H.Q's, "D", "B", "C", "A" Companies, supply and baggage wagons. Transport will move in rear of the Company to which it belongs.

   The Battalion will form up on the LA VIGNETTE - LINSELLES Road, with the head of the column at road junction 200 yards South West of Battalion H.Q's and ready to move off at 10.10 hours.

3. Route. LINSELLES - LEVEAU - QUESNOY - CROIX AU BOIS.

   Road intervals will be the same as for to-days march.

4. Blankets. Blankets (1 blanket per man of Companies and all Bn. H.Q's blankets) will be rolled in bundles of 10, labelled and dumped at the Quartermasters' Stores by 07.30 hours.

5. Dress. Arms, equipment and packs. Waterproof sheets folded and strapped under the flap of the pack. Men not ordered to carry packs will carry waterproof sheets rolled on the back of the belt. Mess tins carried in packs.

6. An Officer of each Company will synchronise watches at Battalion Headquarters at 09.15 hours.

7. O.C. "A" Company will detail 1 Sergt. and 4 men to act as slow moving party, to march in rear of the column.

8. ACKNOWLEDGE.

W P Sawdis

Captain for
Lieut. Colonel,
Commanding 30th Battalion Machine Gun Corps.

Copy No. 1. 89th Infantry Brigade.
2. Commanding Officer.
3. O.C. "A" Company.
4. O.C. "B" "
5. O.C. "C" "
6. O.C. "D" "
7. O.C. "H.Q." "
8. Quartermaster.
9. Medical Officer.
10. R.S.M.
11. File.
12.) War Diary.
13.)
14. Spare.

Appendix 12

SECRET. COPY No.

30th BATTALION MACHINE GUN CORPS ORDER No. 64.

Reference Sheet. HAZEBROUCK 1/100,000

29th November, 1918.

1. The 30th Bn. M.G. Corps will march to BAC ST MAUR area to-morrow, November, 30th, 1918.

2. Order of March. Bn. H.Q's, "C", "A", "D", "B" Companies.
Transport will move as on to-days march.
Companies will form up as follows:-

Bn. H.Q's on QUESNOY - CROIX AU BOIS Road, head of Company at cross roads.
"C" Company on road running South East from CROIX AU BOIS, head of Company at cross roads.
"A" & "D" Companies - personnel on same road as "C" Company. Care must be taken to fall in clear of exits from Transport Lines.
"B" Company on FRELINGHIEN - CROIX AU BOIS Road, head of Company at cross roads.
All Companies will be ready to move at 08.20 hours.

3. Route. LA PREVOTE - HOUPLINES - ARMENTIERES - BAC ST MAUR.
Note. Route will follow 2nd class road from S. in HOUPLINES through U in HOUPLINES.
Road interval as before.

4. Dress. As on to-days march.

5. Blankets. The same number of blankets will be carried as before. They must be dumped at Quartermasters Stores by 08.30 hours.

6. Watches will be synchronised at 07.45 hours.

7. O.C. "B" Company will provide the slow moving party.

8. A halt will be made for dinners from 12.00 hours to 13.00 hours. The usual halt at 11.50 hours will not be made.
"A" & "C" Companies will each prepare dinner for half of the H.Q. personnel.

9. ACKNOWLEDGE.

W. Fawkes
Captain for
Lieut. Colonel,
Commanding 30th Battalion Machine Gun Corps.

Copy No. 1. 89th Infantry Brigade.
2. Commanding Officer.
3. O.C. "A" Company.
4. "B" "
5. "C" "
6. "D" "
7. "H.Q." "
8. Quartermaster.
9. Medical Officer.
10. R.S.M.
11. File.
12.) War Diary.
13.)
14. Spare.

Appendix 11.

<u>SECRET</u>.

<u>COPY No.</u>

<u>30th BATTALION MACHINE GUN CORPS ORDER No. [illegible]</u>.

Reference Map. HAZEBROUCK, 1/100,000. 28th November, 1918.

1. The 30th Bn. M.G. Corps will move to CROIX AU BOIS to-morrow, 29th November.

2. <u>Order of March</u>. Bn. H.Q's, "D", "B", "C", "A" Companies, supply and baggage wagons. Transport will move in rear of the Company to which it belongs.
The Battalion will form up on the LA VIGNETTE - LINSELLES Road, with the head of the column at road junction 200 yards South West of Battalion H.Q's and ready to move off at 10.10 hours.

3. <u>Route</u>. LINSELLES - LEVEAU - QUESNOY - CROIX AU BOIS.

Road intervals will be the same as for to-days march.

4. <u>Blankets</u>. Blankets (1 blanket per man of Companies and all Bn. H.Q's blankets) will be rolled in bundles of 10, labelled and dumped at the Quartermasters' Stores by 07.30 hours.

5. <u>Dress</u>. Arms, equipment and packs. Waterproof sheets folded and strapped under the flap of the pack. Men not ordered to carry packs will carry waterproof sheets rolled on the back of the belt. Mess tins carried in packs.

6. An Officer of each Company will synchronise watches at Battalion Headquarters at 09.15 hours.

7. O.C. "A" Company will detail 1 Sergt. and 4 men to act as slow moving party, to march in rear of the column.

8. ACKNOWLEDGE.

W P Hawkes

Captain for
Lieut. Colonel,
Commanding 30th Battalion Machine Gun Corps.

Copy No. 1. 89th Infantry Brigade.
2. Commanding Officer.
3. O.C. "A" Company.
4. O.C. "B" "
5. O.C. "C" "
6. O.C. "D" "
7. O.C. "H.Q." "
8. Quartermaster.
9. Medical Officer.
10. R.S.M.
11. File.
12.) War Diary.
13.)
14. Spare.

Appendix 12

SECRET. COPY No.

30th BATTALION MACHINE GUN CORPS ORDER No. 64.

Reference Sheet. HAZEBROUCK 1/100,000

29th November, 1918.

1. The 30th Bn. M.G. Corps will march to BAC ST MAUR area to-morrow, November, 30th, 1918.

2. Order of March. Bn. H.Q's, "C", "A", "D", "B" Companies.
Transport will move as on to-days march.
Companies will form up as follows:-

Bn. H.Q's on QUESNOY - CROIX AU BOIS Road, head of Company at cross roads.
"C" Company on road running South East from CROIX AU BOIS, head of Company at cross roads.
"A" & "D" Companies - personnel on same road as "C" Company. Care must be taken to fall in clear of exits from Transport Lines.
"B" Company on FRELINGHIEN - CROIX AU BOIS Road, head of Company at cross roads.
All Companies will be ready to move at 08.20 hours.

3. Route. LA PREVOTE - HOUPLINES - ARMENTIERES - BAC ST MAUR.
Note. Route will follow 2nd class road from S. in HOUPLINES through U in HOUPLINES.
Road interval as before.

4. Dress. As on to-days march.

5. Blankets. The same number of blankets will be carried as before. They must be dumped at Quartermasters Stores by 08.30 hours.

6. Watches will be synchronised at 07.45 hours.

7. O.C. "B" Company will provide the slow moving party.

8. A halt will be made for dinners from 12.00 hours to 13.00 hours. The usual halt at 11.50 hours will not be made.
"A" & "C" Companies will each prepare dinner for half of the H.Q. personnel.

9. ACKNOWLEDGE.

W P Sawdes
Captain for
Lieut. Colonel,
Commanding 30th Battalion Machine Gun Corps.

Copy No. 1. 89th Infantry Brigade.
2. Commanding Officer.
3. O.C. "A" Company.
4. " "B" "
5. " "C" "
6. " "D" "
7. " "H.Q." "
8. Quartermaster.
9. Medical Officer.
10. R.S.M.
11. File.
12.} War Diary.
13.}
14. Spare.

Original

Confidential

V.L. 10

War Diary

of

30th Battalion Machine Gun Corps

For the month of December, 1918.

Volume VII

1-31. December, 1918.

Army Form C. 2118.

WAR DIARY
or
INTELLIGENCE SUMMARY.
(*Erase heading not required.*)

Instructions regarding War Diaries and Intelligence Summaries are contained in F. S. Regs., Part II. and the Staff Manual respectively. Title pages will be prepared in manuscript.

Place	Date	Hour	Summary of Events and Information	Remarks and references to Appendices
St. FLORIS.	1-12-18.		The Battalion moved to St. FLORIS from BAC ST MAUR.	Appendix 1.
STAPLE.	2-12-18		The Battalion moved to STAPLE.	" 2.
	3-12-18. 4-12-18 5-12-18.		The 3rd, 4th & 5th were devoted to cleaning of clothing, equipment, harness, and limbers, and to the construction of Latrines, grease-traps etc. The Companies were at Company Commanders disposal. The following reinforcements joined the Battalion:- 2nd Lieut. P. Williams, (posted to "D" Coy (rejoined from C.C.S.) and 49 other ranks.	
	6-12-18.		The first Battalion parade took place. The Battalion did Bn. Drill under the Commanding Officer. The following reinforcements joined the Battalion:- 2nd Lieut. C.E. Ullathorne (posted to "A" Coy as Transport Officer) and 26 Other ranks. Lieut. T.F. Burke, D.S.O. was transferred from "A" to "C" Coy.	
	7-12-18.		Notice was received that the Commanding Officer, Lieut. Col. H.G.V. Roberts, M.C. had been awarded the Croix de Guerre a l' Ordre (Army).	
	8-12-18.		Church Parades were held for Roman Catholics.	
	9-12-18.		An equitation class for Officers was commenced under 2nd Lieut. Ullathorne.	
	10-12-18.		The usual Battalion Parade was held in the morning. Several inter-section football matches were played during the day in connection with the Inter-Section Competition.	
	11-12-18.		A lecture was delivered to the Battalion by Major F.B. Chevasse, A/D.A.D.M.S., 30th Division. After the lecture Companies were employed on filling in trenches. The first party of Coal Miners proceeded to the Concentration Camp, HAZEBROUCK for demobilization. Fighting Limbers were inspected by the Commanding Officer.	
	12-12-18.		The Battalion Association Team played a team of the 89th Brigade Headquarters, away, Result:- Bn. 3 goals, 89th Brigade H.Q. 2 goals.	
	13-12-18.		Usual Battalion parade took place. The Battalion Rugby Team played a team of the 97th Field Ambulance at home. Result. Bn. 29 Points. 97th Field Ambulance Nil.	
	14-12-18.		In the morning Companies were employed on filling in trenches.	
	15-12-18.		Parade Services were held for Church of England and Roman Catholics denominations. A party of Coal Miners left the Unit for Demobilization.	
	16-12-18.		Battalion Rugby Team played a team of the 7/8th Royal Inniskilling Fusiliers at home. Result.- Bn. 12 Points. 7/8th R. Inniskilling Fus. Nil.	
	17-12-18.		Companies were at Company Commanders disposal. 2 O.R's joined the Battalion from M.G.C. Base Depot. More Coal Miners left the Unit for Demobilization.	
	18-12-18.		Companies were employed on filling in trenches in the morning.	
	19-12-18.		The clothing of all Other ranks of the Battalion ~~were~~ was disinfested in the Foden Disinfestor.	

D. D. & L., London, E.C. (10340) Wt W5300/P713 750,000 3/18 E 2688 Forms/C2118/16.

Instructions regarding War Diaries and Intelligence Summaries are contained in F. S. Regs., Part II. and the Staff Manual respectively. Title pages will be prepared in manuscript.

WAR DIARY
or
INTELLIGENCE SUMMARY.
(Erase heading not required.)

Army Form C. 2118.

Place	Date	Hour	Summary of Events and Information	Remarks and references to Appendices
STAPLE.	20-12-18.		Disinfesting completed. During the morning the Commanding Officer interviewed all Officers.	
	21-12-18.		The Battalion Association Team played at team of the 7/8th R. Inniskilling Fus., away, Result:- Bn. 3 goals. R. Inniskilling Fus. 3 goals.	
	22-12-18.		Parade Services were held for Church of England and Roman Catholics Denominations. Battalion Rugby Team played a team of the 7/8th R. Inniskilling Fus. Result. Bn. 28 Points, R. Inniskilling Fus. Nil.	
	23-12-18.		The Battalion carried out a rehersal of the following day's Ceremonial Parade.	
	24-12-18.		Brig. General Goodman G.O.C. 30th Division inspected the Battalion, and presented Medal ribbons and silver match boxes. The Battalion Association Team played a team of the 101st Bn. M.G.C. at home. Result. 101st Bn. M.G.C. 3 goals. Bn. 1 goals.	
	25-12-18.)		No parades took place on these days, A Y.M.C.A. was opened.	
	26-12-18.)		The Battalion Concert Party gave its first performance on Boxing Day	
	27-12-18.		The Commaning Officer granted this day as a holiday. The Bn. Rugby team played a team of the 2nd Bn. S. Lancs Regt. at home. Result. Bn. Nil. 2nd Bn. S. Lancs. Nil. The Battalion Association Team played a team of the 6th Bn. S.W.B. Result. 6th Bn. S.W.B. 2 goals, Bn. 2 goals.	
	28-12-18.		Companies at Company Commanders disposal.	
	29-12-18.		Parades Services were held for Church of England and Roman Catholics Denominations.	
	30-12-18		Each Company carried out a Route March of about 6 miles.	
	31-12-18.		2 Other Ranks joined the Battalion from M.G.C. Base Depot.	

	O.	O.R.
Strength of the Battalion at December 1st.	52.	843.
Increase (2nd Lt. P. Williams, 2nd Lt. C.E. Ullathorne)	2	99
	54.	942.
Decrease (Lt. G.A. Pemberton, Lt. B.M. Rumbold, Major G.S. Nelson.)	3.	146.
Strength of Battalion at 1st January, 1919.	51.	796.

D. M. Parker, Major for Lieut. Colonel,
Commanding 30th Battalion Machine Gun Corps.

D. D. & L., London, E.C.
(10340) Wt W5300/P713 750,000 3/18 E 2688 Forms/C2118/16.

Original

Confidential

Appendix to War Diary
of
30th Battalion Machine Gun Corps.

For ~~the~~ month of December, 1918.

Volume VIII

1-31-12-18.

SECRET. COPY No. 13 Appendix 31

30th BATTALION MACHINE GUN CORPS ORDER No. 65.

Reference Map. HAZEBROUCK, 1/100,000 30th November, 1918.

1. The 30th Bn. M.G. Corps will march to ST FLORIS to-morrow, December, 1st. 1918.

2. The Battalion will form up as follows:-

(i) Personnel. Personnel will form up on the BAC ST MAUR - ESTAIRES Road, facing West, head of column at the starting point, 300 yards North of the Y in SAILLY, and in the following order of march:-
Bn. H.Q's, "B" Coy, "D" Coy, "C" Coy, "A" Coy.
Personnel of Bn. H.Q's, "A" & "D" Companies will cross the R. LYS by the footbridge by which they crossed it to-day.
Cs' C. these Companies will ensure that a sufficiently early start is made to allow for the crossing of the river in single file.

(ii) Transport. (a) All Field Kitchens and watercarts and Bn. H.Q. Transport will form up immediately in rear of the personnel on the BAC ST MAUR - ESTAIRES Road.
Note. This Transport will move under the command of an Officer to be detailed by O.C. "A" Coy. This Officer will ensure that the field kitchens and watercarts of "D" & "A" Companies, & Bn. H.Q. Transport, are past the cross roads at CROIX Du BAC before limbers of "D" & "A" Companies pass that point.
(b) "B" & "C" Companies limbers will form up on the BAC ST MAUR - ESTAIRES Road, with the head of "B" Company limbers in rear of Bn. H.Q. Transport.
(c) "D" & "A" Companies limbers will form up on the track from CROIX du BAC to BAC ST MAUR, with the head of "D" Company limbers at the junction of this track with BAC ST MAUR - ESTAIRES Road.
Order of march for Transport:- Transport detailed in 2 (a) above, limbers of "B" Coy, "D" Coy, "C" Coy, "A" Coy, baggage wagons.

3. The head of the column will pass the starting point at 07.30 hours.

4. Route. ESTAIRES - LA GORGUE - MERVILLE - ST FLORIS.

5. Road intervals. An interval of 50 yards will be kept between
(a) personnel and field kitchens.
(b) rear of Bn. H.Q. Transport and leading limber of "B" Coy.
(c) limbered transport of each Company.

6. Blankets. The same numbers as on previous days will be carried by G.S. Wagons. Cs' C. "A", "D", Bn.H.Q. Companies will provide a guide for these wagons, to report at Quartermasters Stores at 05.30 hours. Blankets of "C" Company will be dumped on road near billets at 05.45 hours, when they will be picked up by lorry.

7. Dress for the march will be as on to-day's march.

8. Watches will be synchronised at the starting point at 07.20 hours.

9. ACKNOWLEDGE.

W J Hawkes
Captain for
Lieut. Colonel,
Commanding 30th Battalion Machine Gun Corps.

Copy No. 1. 89th Infantry Brigade.
2. Commanding Officer.
3. O.C. "A" Company.
4. O.C. "B" Company.
5. O.C. "C" Company.
6. O.C. "D" Company
7. O.C. H.Q.Company.

Copy No. 8. Quartermaster.
9. Medical Officer.
10. R.S.M.
11. File.
12. War Diary.
13. " "
14. Spare.

SECRET. COPY No. Appendix 2

30th BATTALION MACHINE GUN CORPS ORDER No. 36.

Reference Map, HAZEBROUCK 1/100,000 1st December, 1918.

1. The 30th Bn. M.G. Corps will march to STAPLE to-morrow, December, 2nd. 1918.

2. The Battalion will form up at 07.30 hours with the head of the column at the road junction 200 yards due South of K. in LOCK in the following order of march:-

(a) Personnel of Bn. H.Q's, "A" Coy, "D" Coy, "B" Coy, "C" Coy in that order.
(b) All field kitchens and water carts, and Bn. H.Q transport, in rear of personnel.
(c) Limbered Transport of "A" & "D" Companies on road on which these Companies are billetted, leading limber of "A" Coy at road junction 400 yards due North of first T. in ST. VENANT.
(d) Limbered Transport of "B" & "C" Companies, on road on which those Companies are billetted, leading limber of "B" Coy at the same road junction.
Transport will march in the same order as the personnel of Companies.

3. The same road intervals will be maintained as on to-day's march.

4. Blankets. The same numbers as on previous days will be carried. They will be collected by lorry at Companies H.Q!s at the following times:-

"B" Company - 06.30 hours.
"D" " - 06.50 hours.
Bn. H.Q's. - 07.15 hours.

5. Dress. As for to-day's march.

6. An Officer of each Company will synchronise watches at Bn. H.Q's at 07.30 hours.

7. O.C. "B" Company will detail a slow moving party consisting of an N.C.O. and 4 men to move in rear of the column.

8. Sick parade. will be held at 07.00 hours. N.C.O's and men reporting sick must parade in marching order, ready to proceed with the column, and OC' C. Companies will each detail an N.C.O. to be in charge of the sick of the Company.

9. ACKNOWLEDGE.

W J Sawders
Captain for
Lieut. Colonel,
Commanding 30th Battalion Machine Gun Corps.

Copy No. 1. 89th Infantry Brigade.
2. Commanding Officer.
3. O.C. "A" Company.
4. O.C. "B" "
5. O.C. "C" "
6. O.C. "D" "
7. O.C. "H.Q" "
8. Quartermaster.
9. Medical Officer.
10. R.S.M.
11. File.
12. War Diary.
13. " "
14. Spare.

Confidential

30th Battalion Machine Gun Corps

VR 11

War Diary – Volume. VII January 1919.

Instructions regarding War Diaries and Intelligence Summaries are contained in F. S. Regs., Part II. and the Staff Manual respectively. Title pages will be prepared in manuscript.

WAR DIARY
or
INTELLIGENCE SUMMARY.
(Erase heading not required.)

Army Form C. 2118.

Place	Date	Hour	Summary of Events and Information	Remarks and references to Appendices
	1919.			
STAPLE (HAZEBROUCK) 5a.	Jan.	1st.	New Year's Day observed as a holiday.	
	"	2nd.	Companies at Company Commanders disposal. Publication of Mention in Despatches of Captain W.J. Fawkes, M.C. and R.S.M. Grant, D.C.M., M.M.	
	"	3rd.	Preparations made for move to new camp. Advance party despatched.	
	"	4th.	Battalion moved to LA LACQUE, Near AIRE by march route. Commanding Officer left for one months leave to U.K. Lieut. Barnett and guard left at STAPLE.	APPENDIX 1.
LA LACQUE	"	5th.	Divine Service in the Camp Theatre for C.E. at 11.00 hours. Voluntary Service in Y.M.C.A. at 18.30 hours.	
	"	6th	All Companies carried out improvements to Camp buildings, duck-boards &c.	
	"	7th.	Programme of training carried out. All animals of the Battalion were inspected and classified by Veterinary Board. Lieut. J.O.N. McKenna assumed duties of Adjutant.	
	"	8th	Companies at Company Commanders disposal.	
	"	9th.	Companies attended the Baths.	
	"	10th.	Lecture by Captain G.M. Painter, Education Officer, on "Science and the man in the Street", in the Y.M.C.A. Battalion Rugby team played the R.F.A. Result. R.F.A. 10 pts. Battn. 5 pts. "Optimists" Concert Party in the Camp Theatre.	
	"	11th.	Companies at Company Commanders disposal. "Optimists" show repeated.	
	"	12th.	Divine Service for C.E. in Camp Theatre at 11.00 hours. Divine Service for Nonconformists in Y.M.C.A. at 10.00 hours. Information received of award of Belgian decoration of the CROIX de GUERRE to Major O.M. Parker, Captain P.G. Walsh and C.Q.M.S. H.B. Kincaid.	
	"	13th.	Companies at Company Commanders disposal.	
	"	14th.	" " " "	
	"	15th.	" " " "	
	"	16th.	" " " "	
	"	17th.	Detailed orders issued for moves of Companies.	APPENDIX 2.
	"	18th.	The Battalion, less "D" Company left LA LACQUE, personnel proceeding by train and Transport by road to the following destinations:- "A" Company to ETAPLES. "B" Company to AUDRICQ. "C" Company to BOULOGNE Battn. H.Q's to AMBLETEUSE near BOULOGNE.	

D. D. & L., London, E.C. (10340) Wt W5300/P713 750,000 3/18 E 2688 Forms/C2118/16.

Instructions regarding War Diaries and Intelligence Summaries are contained in F. S. Regs., Part II. and the Staff Manual respectively. Title pages will be prepared in manuscript.

WAR DIARY
or
INTELLIGENCE SUMMARY.
(*Erase heading not required.*)

Army Form C. 2118.

Place	Date	Hour	Summary of Events and Information	Remarks and references to Appendices
	Jan.	19th.	"D" Company left LA LACQUE for DUNKIRK.	
AMBLETEUSE.	"	20th.	Battalion Headquarters and Companies reached their several destinations. "A" Company were accommodated in No. 3. Employment Base Depot, ETAPLES. "B" " " " " No. 9. Camp, AUDRICQ. "D" " " " " No. 2. Camp, DUNKIRK. Bn. H.Q's. " " " No. 1. Reinforcement Camp, AMBLETEUSE. "C" Company " " with ½ Company at PONT de BRICQUES. and ½ " " POINTE aux OIES.	
	Jan. to Jan.	21st to 31st.	From this date, Companies were employed on Prisoners of War Escort Duty under the orders of the BASE COMMANDANTS of the places at which they were stationed. Battalion Headquarters remained at AMBLETEUSE, Commanding Officer was appointed O.C. Details Wing of the Camp, accommodation being provided for the 89th Infantry Brigade Transport and for details of 21st Infantry Brigade Headquarters.	

D. M. Parker
Major,
Commanding 30th Battalion Machine Gun Corps.

D. D. & L., London, E.C.
(10340) Wt W5300/P713 750,000 3/18 E 2688 Forms/C2118/16.

Confidential

30th Bn Machine Gun Corps

V8

Appendices to

War diary

Vol. VII January 1919

Appendix I

SECRET. COPY No. 15.

30th BATTALION MACHINE GUN CORPS ORDER No. 68.

Reference Sheet. HAZEBROUCK 5a. 1/100,000.
CALAIS. 13. 1/100,000. 17th January, 1919.

1. The Battalion less "D" Company will move to-morrow the 18th January, 1919 as under, Personnel proceeding by train, transport by road.

Battalion Headquarters & "C" Company to BOULOGNE.
"A" Company to ETAPLES.
"B" " to AUDRICQ.

"A"

2. Personnel will entrain at AIRE to-morrow at 16.00 hours and will form up on road south side of Camp.
Starting point will be Canal Bridge.
Head of column will pass the starting point at 15.15 hours.

Order of March. "A" Company.
Battalion Headquarters.
"C" Company.
"B" "

Intervals. Five minutes interval will be maintained between Companies.
Dress. Full Marching Order.
Waggons. 2 G.S. Waggons have been allotted to each Company and 4 to Battalion Headquarters. These waggons will be loaded and despatched so as to reach AIRE Station by 11.00 hours and 15.00 hours.

Loading Parties. "A", "B" & "C" Companies will each provide a loading party of 1 N.C.O. and 10 men and "D" Company will provide a loading party of 2 N.C.O's and 20 men. These parties will report to Lieut. Duncan at 10.30 hours at AIRE STATION.
A similar party will report at 14.30 hours.
Companies will make their own arrangements for loading G.S. waggons at this end.

Lamps & Washbowls will be handed into the Quartermasters Stores by 09.00 hours to-morrow.
Plates will be returned to Y.M.C.A. by 14.00 hours to-morrow.
Any deficiencies will be charged for at the rate of 2 francs per plate.
O.C. "D" Company will make his own arrangements with the Y.M.C.A.

Huts. Company Commanders are responsible that their huts and Company lines are left clean. Certificate to this effect will be rendered to Battalion Orderly Room by 14.00 hours.

"B"

Transport will move by road to-morrow as follows:-

"A" Company will move off at 09.30 hours.
Staging will be as follows:-

Night 18/19. COYECQUE. Billets to be obtained from Area Commandant, COYECQUE.
" 19/20. HERLY-AVESNES. Billets to be obtained from Area Commandant, VERCHOCQ
" 20/21. MONT CAVREL. Billets to be obtained from Area Commandant, MONT CAVREL.

P.T.O.

"B" Company will move off at 10.00 hours.
Staging will be as follows:-

Night 18/19. ARQUES. Billets to be obtained from Area Commandant, ARQUES.
" 19/20. NORDAUSQUES. Billets to be obtained from Area Commandant, NORDAUSQUES.

"C" Company & Headquarters will move off at 09.45 hours.
Staging will be as follows:-

Night 18/19 OUVE-WIRQUIN. Billets to be obtained from Area Commandant, OUVE-WIRQUIN.
" 19/20 DESVRES. Billets to be obtained from Area Commandant, DESVRES.

Rations. Each Company Transport will carry rations and fodder for 18th & 19th. "B", "C" & "H.Q" Companies will collect rations and fodder for the 20th and "A" Company for the 20th & 21st from the Supply Dump, AIRE on route to-morrow.

"C"

Battalion Headquarters will close at LA LACQUE at 15.00 hours and open at BOULOGNE on arrival.

3. ACKNOWLEDGE.

Lieut. for
Major,
Commanding 30th Battalion Machine Gun Corps.

Copy No. 1. C.R.A. 30th Brit. Div.
2. 30th British Division.
3. Commanding Officer.
4. O.C. "A" Company.
5. O.C. "B" "
6. O.C. "C" "
7. O.C. "D" "
8. O.C. "H.Q." "
9. Transport Officer "A" Coy.
10. " " "B" "
11. " " "C" "
12. " " "D" "
13. Quartermaster.
14. File.
15. War Diary,
16. " "
17. Spare.

Appendix II

SECRET. COPY No. 16

30th. Battalion Machine Gun Corps Order No. 37.

Reference Sheet HAZEBROUCK 5 A. 3rd. January, 1919.

1. The 30th. Battalion Machine Gun Corps will move to camp at LA LACQUE, near AIRE tomorrow, 4th. January, 1919, by march route.

2. The Starting Point will be on the road outside the Battalion Parade Ground, head of the column at the entrance to the ground.
Order of March, Personnel, "H.Q." "A" "B" "C" "D" Coy,
followed by Transport, (1) Field kitchens & Water carts, & HQ Transport.
(2) Limbered Transport of Coys in same order as personnel.
(3) Baggage & Supply Wagons.
Time of passing starting point will be 10-00 hours.

3. DRESS. Battle Order will be worn, and drivers will wear greatcoats.

4. Road Intervals. Between personnel of Coys. - - - 10 Yards.
Between every 12 vehicles, - - - 50 Yards.

5. BLANKETS. O's C. "H.Q" "A" and "B" Companies will arrange for all blankets of their Coys to be rolled in bundles of 10 and dumped in the Concert Hall by 08.00 hours.
A G.S. wagon will report at each of "C" and "D" Coys for the blankets of those Coys at 08.00 hours.

6. Transport of Stores. Any tables and forms in possession of Coys which they are unable to carry on their own transport will be concentrated in the Concert Hall by 08.00 hours.
All kit, rations and stores of "H.Q" Coy will be dumped at the same place by 08.00 hours.
Athletic gear will be conveyed in the 'bus reporting at Battalion Headquarters at 09.00 hours.

7. GUARD. O.C. "D" Coy will detail 1 N.C.O. and 5 men to guard stores left behind. This guard will come under the orders of Lieut. H.J.Barnett who will continue to act as Area Commandant until further orders. The guard will be rationed up to the 5th inclusive and will parade in full marching order at Battalion Headquarters at 08.00 hours tomorrow.

8. BILLETS. Coy Commanders will ensure that billets are left clean and will forward a certificate to this effect to Battalion Orderly Room by 09.00 hours.

9. Battalion Headquarters will close at STAPLE at 09.00 hours and reopen at LA LACQUE on arrival.

10. Please acknowledge.

W. J. [illegible]
Captain for
Lieut. Colonel,
Commanding 30th Battalion Machine Gun Corps.

Copy No. 1. 30th Brit. Div. "G".
2. " " " "A" & "Q"
3. " Divl. Train.
4. Commanding Officer.
5. Second in Command.
6. O.C. "A" Company.
7. "B" "
8. "C" "
9. "D" "
10. "H.Q." "

Copy No. 11. Lieut. Barnett.
12. Battn T.O.
13. Quartermaster.
14. Signalling Sergt.
15. File.
16. War Diary.
17. War Diary.

Instructions regarding War Diaries and Intelligence Summaries are contained in F. S. Regs., Part II. and the Staff Manual respectively. Title pages will be prepared in manuscript.

WAR DIARY
or
INTELLIGENCE SUMMARY.
(Erase heading not required.)

30 Bn M G Corps

12

Army Form C. 2118.

Place	Date	Hour	Summary of Events and Information	Remarks and references to Appendices
AMBLETEUSE.	Feb. 1st	1919. -	Bn H.Q.'s at AMBLETEUSE, Companies located as follows;- "A" Company at ETAPLES. "B" " " AUDRUICQ. "C" " " WIMEREUX and ECHINGHEN. "D" " " DUNKIRK	
			Throughout the month, Companies were employed on Prisoner of War Escort duties at the several Bases at which they were accomodated. Bn H.Q's moved to ST LEONARDS, south of Boulogne, on the 6th, and were still there at the end of the month, this constituting the only move of the Battalion.	
ST LEONARDS, (BOULOGNE)	28th.	-	Strength ofnthe Battalion Feb.1st. Officers. 50. O.R's. 723. " " " " Feb.28th. 38. 417. Decrease. 12 306.	

A. Hoo

Major,
Commanding 30th Battalion Machine Gun Corps.

D. D. & L., London, E.C.
(10340) Wt W5300/P713 750,000 3/18 E 2688 Forms/C2118/16.

War Diary

-of-

30th Bn Machine Gun Corps

-for-

February 1919

30TH
BATTALION,
MACHINE GUN CORPS.
No. G. 900
Date 17.4.19

Headquarters,
30th. British Division "G"

Herewith War Diary for the month of March 1919, please.

HEAD QUARTERS
No. CR/515.L.
17 APR 1919
30th DIVISION

17/4/19.

Captain for Lt-Col.,
Commanding 30th. Battalion Machine Gun Corps.

"A"

Passed

[illegible]

18/4/19

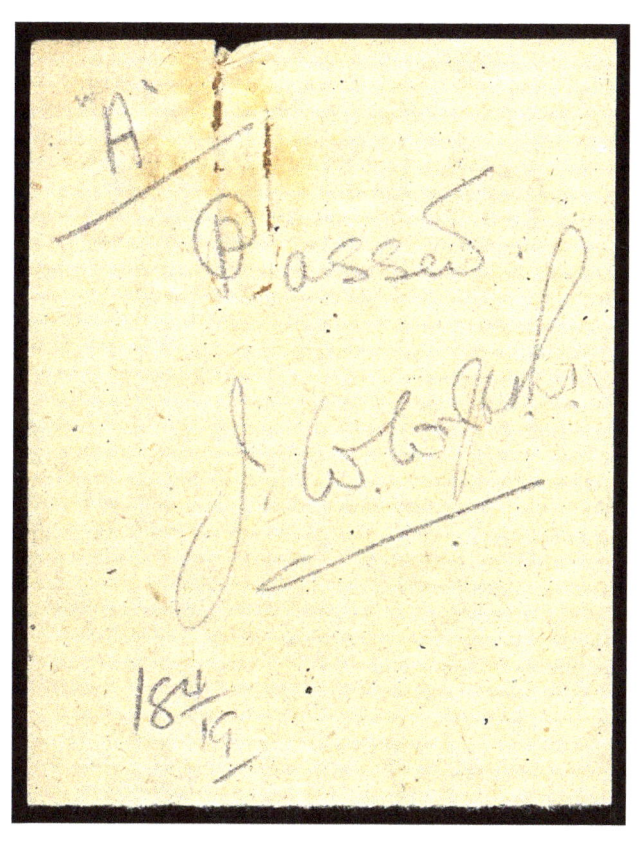

Instructions regarding War Diaries and Intelligence Summaries are contained in F. S. Regs., Part II. and the Staff Manual respectively. Title pages will be prepared in manuscript.

WAR DIARY
or
INTELLIGENCE SUMMARY.
(Erase heading not required.)

Army Form C. 2118.

Vol 13

Place	Date	Hour	Summary of Events and Information	Remarks and references to Appendices
ST. LEONARDS.	March 1st.		Bn. H.Qs. at St.LEONARDS, Companies located as follows;- "A" Company at ETAPLES. "B" " " AUDRUICQ. "C" " " WIMEREUX. & ECHINGHEN. "D" " " DUNKIRK.	
	5th.		"B" Company moved to ECHINGHEN.	
	13th.		"D" Company moved to HENRIVILLE. Transport to ECHINGHEN.	
	27th.		Drafts arrived from 14th. and 36th. Bns. M.G.C.	
	28th.		Draft " " 17th. Bn.	
			During the period March 1st - 28th. Companies continued carrying out Prisoners of War Escort Duties.	
	29th.		The Battalion concentrated at No.4 Large Rest Camp, HENRIVILLE. Transport at ECHINGHEN	
	30th.		Detachments left to relieve detachments of 2/4th.ROYAL BERKSHIRE REGT.	
	31st.		Further detachments sent out, thereby completing relief of 2/4th. ROYAL BERKSHIRE REGT.	
			Strength of Battalion, March 1st. 38 Offs.417 O.Rs. March 31st. 56 " 716 " Increase 18 Officers.299 O.Rs.	
			A.G. Roberts Lieutenant-Colonel, Commanding 30th.Battalion Machine Gun Corps.	

D. D. & L., London, E.C.
(10340) Wt W5300/P713 750,000 3/18 E 2688 Forms/C2118/16.

Instructions regarding War Diaries and Intelligence Summaries are contained in F. S. Regs., Part II. and the Staff Manual respectively. Title pages will be prepared in manuscript.

WAR DIARY
or
INTELLIGENCE SUMMARY.
(*Erase heading not required.*)

Army Form C. 2118.

Place	Date	Hour	Summary of Events and Information	Remarks and references to Appendices
ST. LEONARDS.	March 1st.		Bn. H.Qs. at St.LEONARDS, Companies located as follows;- "A" Company at ETAPLES. "B" " " AUDRUICQ. "C" " " WIMEREUX. & ECHINGHEN. "D" " " DUNKIRK.	
	5th.		"B" Company moved to ECHINGHEN.	
	13th.		"D" Company moved to HENRIVILLE. Transport to ECHINGHEN.	
	27th.		Drafts arrived from 14th. and 36th. Bns. M.G.C.	
	28th.		Draft " " 17th. Bn.	
			During the period March 1st - 28th. Companies continued carrying out Prisoners of War Escort Duties.	
	29th.		The Battalion concentrated at No.4 Large Rest Camp, HENRIVILLE. Transport at ECHINGHEN	
	30th.		Detachments left to relieve detachments of 2/4th.ROYAL BERKSHIRE REGT.	
	31st.		Further detachments sent out, thereby completing relief of 2/4th. ROYAL BERKSHIRE REGT.	
			Strength of Battalion, March 1st. 38 Offs.417 O.Rs. March 31st. 56 " 716 " Increase 18 Officers.299 O.Rs.	

[signature]

Lieutenant-Colonel,
Commanding 30th.Battalion Machine Gun Corps.

D. D. & L., London, E.C.
(10340) Wt W5300/P713 750,000 3/18 E 2688 Forms/C2118/16.

Instructions regarding War Diaries and Intelligence Summaries are contained in F. S. Regs., Part II. and the Staff Manual respectively. Title pages will be prepared in manuscript.

WAR DIARY
or
INTELLIGENCE SUMMARY.
(Erase heading not required.)

Army Form C. 2118.

Place	Date	Hour	Summary of Events and Information	Remarks and references to Appendices
ST. LEONARDS.	March 1st.		Bn. H.Qs. at St.LEONARDS, Companies located as follows;- "A" Company at ETAPLES. "B" " " AUDRUICQ. "C" " " WIMEREUX. & ECHINGHEN. "D" " " DUNKIRK.	
	5th.		"B" Company moved to ECHINGHEN.	
	13th.		"D" Company moved to HENRIVILLE. Transport to ECHINGHEN.	
	27th.		Drafts arrived from 14th. and 56th. Bns. M.G.C.	
	28th.		Draft " " 17th. Bn.	
			During the period March 1st - 28th. Companies continued carrying out Prisoners of War Escort Duties.	
	29th.		The Battalion concentrated at No.4 Large Rest Camp, HENRIVILLE. Transport at ECHINGHEN	
	30th.		Detachments left to relieve detachments of 2/4th.ROYAL BERKSHIRE REGT.	
	31st.		Further detachments sent out, thereby completing relief of 2/4th. ROYAL BERKSHIRE REGT.	
			Strength of Battalion, March 1st. 38 Offs.417 O.Rs. March 31st. 56 " 716 " Increase 18 Officers.299 O.Rs.	
			[illegible signature] Lieutenant-Colonel, Commanding 20th. Battalion Machine Gun Corps.	

D. D. & L., London, E.C.
(10340) Wt W5300/P713 750,000 3/18 E 2688 Forms/C2118/16.

Instructions regarding War Diaries and Intelligence Summaries are contained in F. S. Regs., Part II. and the Staff Manual respectively. Title pages will be prepared in manuscript.

WAR DIARY
or
~~INTELLIGENCE SUMMARY~~.
(Erase heading not required.)

Army Form C. 2118.

Vol 14

Place	Date	Hour	Summary of Events and Information	Remarks and references to Appendices
HENRIVILLE.	1st. April.		Battalion at No.4 LARGE REST CAMP, HENRIVILLE, Transport at ECHINGHEN.	
	4th.		Transport moved from ECHINGHEN to No.3 VETERINARY HOSPITAL, ST.LEONARDS.	
	8th.		Transport moved from ST.LEONARDS to HENRIVILLE.	
	21st.		Lieut-Colonel ROBERTS, Captains McKENNA & DUNCAN, Lts. BARTLEY, WHEATLEY, JENKINS, and MOORE proceeded to ENGLAND with DIVISIONAL RUGBY XV.	
	27th.		DIVISIONAL RUGBY XV returned.	
			During the month the whole Battalion was employed on BASE DUTIES. Detachments being at OUTREAU, BASSIN LOUBET, FAUQUEMBERGUES, and COLUMN CAMP, doing duties as guards, police, etc.	
			Troops leisure hours filled with football and hockey, several good concerts given for them in the evenings.	
			Strength of the Battalion April 1st. 59 Offs. 726 O.Rs. 30th. 58 Offs. 716 O.Rs.	
			H J Roberts Lieutenant-Colonel, Commanding 30th.Battalion Machine Gun Corps.	

D. D. & L., London, E.C.
(10340) Wt W5300/P713 750,000 3/18 E 2688 Forms/C2118/16.

Headquarters,

30th. Division "G".

HEAD QUARTERS
No. CR 1395
2 JUN 1919
30TH DIVISION

30TH BATTALION, MACHINE GUN CORPS.
No. G/949
Date 1-6-19

Herewith War Diary of this unit for the month of MAY.

1/6/1919.

John McKenna Lt
for Lieutenant-Colonel,
Commanding 30th. Battalion Machine Gun Corps.

Instructions regarding War Diaries and Intelligence Summaries are contained in F. S. Regs., Part II. and the Staff Manual respectively. Title pages will be prepared in manuscript.

WAR DIARY

or

~~INTELLIGENCE SUMMARY~~.

(Erase heading not required.)

Army Form C. 2118.

98/5

Place	Date	Month	Summary of Events and Information	Remarks and references to Appendices
Henriville.	1st.	May.	Battalion at HENRIVILLE CAMP, Le Portel.	
			The Battalion was employed on the same duties as in previous month. Viz:- Base Duties, Detachments were on duty at OUTREAU, BASSIN LOUBET, FAUQUEMBERGUES, & COLUMN CAMP. Whenever possible Cricket was played after Parade hours and in evenings, Whist Drives, and Sing-Songs were organised as often as possible which were well enjoyed. Dances were held once per week from 6 pm. till 10 pm.	
	18th.		12 Officers proceeded to U.K. for Demobilisation.	
	25th.		11 Officers proceeded to U.K. for Demobilisation.	
	30th.		1 Officer. proceeded to U.K. for Demobilisation.	
			Strength of Battalion 1st. May. 58 Officers. 716 O.Ranks.	
			Strength of Battalion 31st.May. 50 Officers. 706 O.Ranks.	

[signature]

Lieutenant-Colonel,
Commanding 30th.Battalion Machine Gun Corps.

D. D. & L., London, E.C.
(10340) Wt W5300/P713 750,000 3/18 E 2688 Forms/C2118/16.

30TH
BATTALION,
MACHINE GUN CORPS.
No. ....
Date. ....

HEAD QUARTERS
OR 2054
3 - JUL 1919
30TH DIVISION

Headquarters.

30th Division "G"

Herewith War Diary of this Unit for the month of June.

7/7/19. [signature] Major.
Commanding 30th Battalion Machine Gun Corps.

Instructions regarding War Diaries and Intelligence Summaries are contained in F. S. Regs., Part II. and the Staff Manual respectively. Title pages will be prepared in manuscript.

WAR DIARY

or

~~INTELLIGENCE SUMMARY.~~

(Erase heading not required.)

Army Form C. 2118.

Vol 16

Place	Date	Hour	Summary of Events and Information	Remarks and references to Appendices
ECAULT.	June 1st		From the 1st June to the 7th June the Battalion was employed on Base Duties, at Boulogne, detachments being stationed at Outreau, Bassin Loubet, Fauquembergues, and Column Camp, the troops leisure hours being catered for with cricket and concerts in the evenings.	
	7th		The Battalion was relieved by the 6th Bn. S.W.B., and moved from HENRIVILLE CAMP, to No. 10 Convalescent Camp, ECAULT, for Intensive Training. Training was carried out daily from 08.30 hours to 13.00 hours. Recreational Training was carried out in the afternoons e.g. Cricket, and entertainments for the evenings included Sing-Songs, Dances, Cinema Shows and Concerts. Inter-Company drill and Inter-Section and Transport Competitions were instuted on the Championship basis, challenge cups being contested for weekly.	
	14th		A Small-Pox Isolation Camp was started upon the arrival of 700 contacts from KANTARA, rations and cooking facilities for the men being provided by the E.F.C. The draft proceeded for Demobilization to St. Martins Camp, on the 17th June.	
	22nd		Two detachments were despatched as follows:- No.1 Detachment. 4 Officers 120 O.Rs to G.H.Q. WIMEREUX, for general duties. No.2 Detachment. 4 Officers 180 O.Rs to BASSIN LOUBET, for Train Guard Duties. The only troops left in camp, consisted of;- (1) Regimental Employ. (2) Transport Personnel.	
	24th		Second draft of contacts arrived in Isolation Camp, Same Routine and Administration existed. Draft despatched to St. Martins Camp, on 25th & 26th. Daily Transport Limber Drill carried out, & Transport Competition Inspection weekly. Strength of Battalion: 1st June. 50 Offs. 706 O.Rs. x " " " 30th June. 45 " 682 " [signature] Major. Commanding 30 th Battalion Machine Gun Corps.	

D. D. & L., London, E.C.
(10340) Wt W5300/P713 750,000 3/18 E 2688 Forms/C2118/16.

Headquarters.
30th Division "G"

Herewith please find War Diary in respect of 30th Bn. Machine Gun Corps, for the month of July 1919.

W. Smetham Hutton
Lieut for
Captain for
Lieut-Colonel.

4/8/1919. Commanding 30th Battalion Machine Gun Corps.

Instructions regarding War Diaries and Intelligence Summaries are contained in F. S. Regs., Part II. and the Staff Manual respectively. Title pages will be prepared in manuscript.

WAR DIARY
or
~~INTELLIGENCE SUMMARY.~~
(Erase heading not required.)

Army Form C. 2118.

98/17

Place	Date	Hour	Summary of Events and Information	Remarks and references to Appendices
ECAULT.	1st		Owing to the Detachment that went out from this Battalion, the greater part of men in Camp belonged to the Transport who have done a certain amount of Transport Drill each day.	
			Battalion Headquarters and Battalion Transport were located at Ecault Camp, "A" "C" and "D" Companies formed the Train Guard Detachment at Bassin Loubet. "B" Company was employed on G.H.Q. duties with the Camp Commandant, Wimereux.	
	15th		"B" Company less 7 Officers and 56 Other Ranks returned to Ecault Camp.	
			Entertainments were provided for the menby the Camp Cinema, Sing-Songs, Dances and also visiting Concert Parties.	
			Strength on 1/7/1919 45 Officers. 681 Other Ranks. " " 31/7/1919 44 " 674 " "	
			[signature] Lieutenant-Colonel. Commanding 30th Battalion Machine Gun Corps.	

D. D. & L., London, E.C.
(10340) Wt W5300/P713 750,000 3/18 E 2688 Forms/C2118/16.

SECRET.

SUBJECT - War Diaries of 30th Bn. Machine Gun Corps.

A/23899.

Secretary,
War Office (S.D.2.)
LONDON.

Herewith War Diaries of the 30th Battalion Machine Gun Corps for the months of August and September 1919.

A M W Mason Capt

BOULOGNE DISTRICT.
22nd October, 1919.
MJ.

Brigadier General.
Commdt. BOULOGNE DISTRICT.

BASE COMMANDANT'S OFFICE.
BOULOGNE.
A
16 OCT 1919
No. 23899

30TH
BATTALION,
MACHINE GUN CORPS.
No. 7/1904
Date 13.10.19

Headquarters,

Boulogne Base,

France.

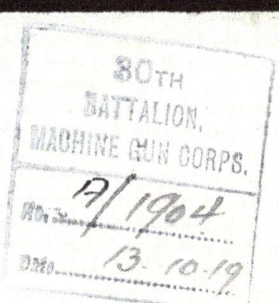

Herewith War Diary of this unit for months of August and September 1919, for disposal please,.

Captain,

Commanding 30th Battalion M.G.C. Cadre.

Harrowby Camp,

Grantham.

12/10/1919.

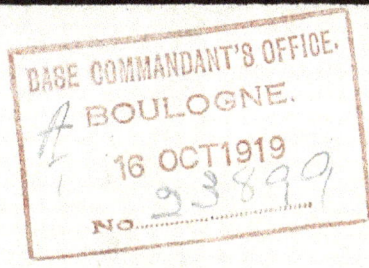

Instructions regarding War Diaries and Intelligence Summaries are contained in F. S. Regs., Part II. and the Staff Manual respectively. Title pages will be prepared in manuscript.

WAR DIARY

or

~~INTELLIGENCE SUMMARY.~~

(Erase heading not required.)

Army Form C. 2118.

Place	Date	Hour	Summary of Events and Information	Remarks and references to Appendices
Ecault Camp. Boulogne.	Sept. 1st.		Battalion Stationed at Ecault Camp.	
	4th.		118 Animals hand d into Remount Depot.	
	10th		Orders received for Battalion to proceed to U.K. on 12th inst. taking only Guns and personal equipment.	
	11th		All remaining animals haded into Remount Depot.	
	12th		The Battalion proceeded to Boulogne with Guns and personal equipment, and embarked for Folkestone. Embarkation strength 27 Officers - 334 Other Ranks. An Equipment Guard of 2 Officers and 20 others ranks was left at Ecault Camp to hand in stores to Ordnance Depot and to rejoin Battalion in U.K. on completion of duty. On arrival at Folkestone, Battalion proceeded to spend night in Cherry Garden Rest Camp, Shorncliffe, where all demobilizable Officers and other ranks were demobilized.	
Shorncliffe.	13th		The rest of the Battalion entrained 11.00 hours 13th September at Shorncliffe and proceeded to Grantham. Entraining strength 14 Officers and 37 other ranks. On arrival at Grantham, proceeded to Harrowby Camp.	
	18th		Battalion reduced to Cadre consisting of 2 Officers and 6 other ranks. Remaining Officers and other ranks and all personnel reporting from leave, hospital etc. taken on the strength of the Receiving Depot, Harrowby Camp.	

Captain.

Commanding 30th Battalion M.G.C. Cadre.

Harrowby Camp,
Grantham.

D. D. & L., London, E.C.
(10340) Wt W5300/P713 750,000 3/18 E 2688 Forms/C2118/16.

www.ingramcontent.com/pod-product-compliance
Lightning Source LLC
Chambersburg PA
CBHW081357160426
43192CB00013B/2428
* 9 7 8 1 4 7 4 5 1 5 2 6 9 *